CU00485760

Shortcut To Ielts Writing

The Ultimate Guide To Immediately Increase Your Ielts Writing Scores

JOHNNY CHUONG

ISBN: 9781520345086

TABLE OF CONTENT

INTRODUCTION

Thank you and congratulate you for downloading the book *"Shortcut To Ielts Writing: The Ultimate Guide To Immediately Increase Your Ielts Writing Scores"* This book will guide you step by step through the grading of the IELTS test. Provide you key structures, tips, grammars, academic vocabularies and essential skills needed to be successful in your IELTS writing. This book not only offers you more than just sample answers, but it also shows you the structure for each task type for BOTH Task 1 and Task 2.

As the author of the book, I promise this book will help you understand IELTS better from different perspectives, walk you step by step and show you how to write for IELTS excellently, so you could improve your IELTS writing band score and even accomplish your goals to receive a band 9!

Thank you again for purchasing this book, and I hope you enjoy it.

Let's get started!

ACADEMIC WRITING PREPARATION

There are two tasks in Academic Writing test: **Task 1** and **Task 2**.

- In Academic IELTS writing **Task 1**, all candidates are asked to describe information presented in a particular graph (bar, line or pie graph), table, chart, or process (how something works, how something is done) and to present the description in their own words. Candidates are required to write at least 150 words which are approximately from 10 to you 15 sentences (200 words suggested maximum). Writing task 1 accounts for 1/3 of your total writing score.

- In Academic IELTS writing **Task 2**, all candidates are required to formulate and develop a position in relation to a given prompt in the form of a question or statement. Ideas should be supported by evidence, and examples may be drawn from the candidates' own experience. Responses must be at least 250 words in length (300 words suggested maximum). Writing task 2 accounts for 2/3 of your total writing score.

IELTS WRITING TASK 1

Task 1 Writing Structure

Task 1 writing structure includes 4 paragraphs:

1.   Introduction: short and simple, just simply paraphrase the questions (rewrite it in your own words).

2.   Overview paragraph: describe 2 main general points. Don't give any figure in this paragraph, save it for the detail paragraphs later.

3.   Detail paragraph 1 + 2: describe the chart from general to a specific order.

Task 1 Band Scores and Marking Criteria

The IELTS examiner will mark you on:

- Task Achievement (25%)

- Coherence and Cohesion (25%)

- Lexical Resource (25%)

- Grammatical Range and Accuracy (25%)

The examiner will give you a band score for each individual criterion above and then your final score for writing task 1 is the average of the 4.

1. Task Achievement / Task Response:

• How well you answer all parts of the task

• You must focus on key points and support every point with evidence.

• Meet the required words count (at least 150 words)

2. Coherence and Cohesion:

• How well-organized your writing is, how well it flows from beginning to end

• Paragraphing and correctly use of words like "however" and "in addition" are essential. Your ideas must be clear and there should be a logical progression from beginning to end.

3. Lexical Resource (vocabulary)

• How varied, accurate and appropriate your use of vocabulary is (don't repeat the words, bring academic vocabularies in your writing by using adjectives and adverbs)

• Your spelling must be correct (minimize errors in spelling and word formation). Demonstrating the ability to paraphrase and use high-level vocabulary correctly is important.

4. Grammatical Range and Accuracy

• How varied, accurate and appropriate your use of grammar is

• Using a wide range of sentence structures will help your writing more academically (using complex sentences with both dependent and independent clauses). Of course, you will not get a high score if you make basic grammar errors (e.g. Verb endings, plurals, etc.). Have a control of using punctuation (commas, periods), understand when and how to use it correctly.

ADVICE

• Spend plenty of time practicing sentence structures: many of the same structures are useful for an IELTS writing tasks.

• Spend extra time writing your first reports and essays. This will allow you to use a new language effectively. But by the end of the course, you need to complete every Task 1 report within 20 minutes, and every Task 2 report within 40 minutes. There is no extra time. In the exam and if you don't finish a piece of writing you will lose a lot of marks.

• These time limits result in our maximum word limits. This is not an IELTS rule, but it is important. In Task 1, for example, you will never be able to write 250 words of good English in 20 minutes. Writing too much is a sign that you are not thinking enough, not producing your best language, or else spending too long producing one of the pieces of writing instead of organizing your time effectively. There are no extra marks for going 100 words over the minimum.

• Because Task 2 is worth more marks than Task 1, it's a good idea to write Task 2 first in the exam. This means that if you run out of time, you will still finish the most important piece of writing. Remember, though, that you will only get a high writing score if you complete both pieces of writing to a high standard. So work hard on time management when preparing for the exam.

• Work on your grammar weaknesses at home. You cannot afford to lose easy marks because of low- level mistakes with elementary grammar (e.g. singular/plural, articles, verb tense, basic prepositions, etc.)

• When you hand an essay in, that is not the end. Your teacher will return your essay and give you feedback. Use that feedback to re-write your essay, then submit it to your teacher again! This requires more work, but it's the best way to improve your writing.

• Do not hand in an essay you copied from a friend, the internet, or even from a model essay written by a teacher in your class. This is called plagiarism. It's cheating, and it will not help you to get a better score in the exam. Your teacher will know if you do this, so don't try it.

SOME USEFUL WORDS FOR REWRITING THE STATEMENT

- Table = chart

- Chart = (could be) line graph, bar chart, a pie chart.

- Show = give = reveal = describe = illustrate = ("compare" if the graph is comparing)

- The diagram = the figure

- Maps show = diagrams illustrate

- The total number = the overall number

- Proportion = percentage

- Information = data

- The proportion of = the number of = the figure for

- (Year) from ... To ... = between ... And ... = over a period of (10,ect) years.

- Shows = illustrates (or 'compares' if the graph is comparing)

- Give information about = show data about

- Compare…..in terms of….

- The chart(s) compare(s) + countries + in terms of + finish the sentence

- The number of = the figure for

- The proportion of = the figure for = the percentage of

- In three countries = in the UK, France and Spain (i.e. Name the countries) = in three different countries = in three countries namely….

- From 1999 to 2009 = between 1999 and 2009 = over a period of 10 years/over a 10 year-period

- In 1999 = in the year 1999

- In 1980 and 2000 = over two separate years/ figures are given for 1980 and 2000/ in two different years.

- Children = youngsters = the young = young people

- The elderly = elderly people = senior citizens

- Average weekly spending = weekly spending figures = spent per week = expenditure per week

- The English = English people

- The Turkish = Turkish people

- The Spanish = Spanish people

- The Swedish = Swedish people

- The Irish = Irish people

- Levels of unemployment = Unemployment rate = Level of joblessness = The proportion of people without job = The proportion of people who were unemployed = The proportion of people who were jobless

- Poverty rate = Level of poverty = The percentage of people who live in poverty = The percentage of people who live under the poverty line = Poverty level

- Sales = turnover

- Per person = per capita

- Annual = yearly = per year

- Per week = weekly = each week = a week

- Spending = expenditure

- Be spent on = be allocated for = be used for = be expended = be paid out for

- The number of people who use cars = The number of people driving to work = The number of car commuters = The number of people who commute by car = The number of people who travel by car = The number of car users

- The number of people who cycle to work = the number of cycling commuters

- Consumption = be used, be consumed, be drunk or be eaten

- Production = manufacture = be produced = be made = be manufactured

- Annual expenditures = yearly spending

- Cell phone services = mobile phones

- Residential services = landline phones

NOTE

Number

- "The number of + plural noun" e.g. the number of students/teachers.

- Don't use "the number of" to describe uncountable nouns or percentages e.g. the number of 20%, 50%, the number of water, coffee, money.

Amount

- Use "the amount of + uncountable noun" e.g. the amount of time/information/money.

- Don't use "the amount of" with countable nouns e.g. the amount of person/people.

Proportion

- Use "the proportion of + plural noun" e.g. the proportion of students, Americans go on to higher education…

- Only use "proportion" to describe percentages (not for numbers).

Figure

- Use "the figure for + plural noun" e.g. the figure for visitors to Japan"

- Use "the figure for" with uncountable nouns e.g. the figure for sugar, electricity, unemployment.

- Use "the figure for" with countries e.g. the figure for UK, US, Canada.

- Use "the figure for" with percentages e.g. the figure (for...) rose to 20%.

INTRODUCTORY EXPRESSIONS

• The graph shows (information about) /indicates /illustrates /highlight (the data about)…

• It is clear from the graph (that)

• As is shown by the graph

• It can be seen from the graph,

• As can be clearly seen from the graph,

• From the graph, it is clear (that)

• As is illustrated by the graph,

VOCABULARY FOR THE INTRODUCTION PART

Starting	Presentation Type	Verb	Description
The given/ The presented/ The shown / The supplied / The provided	diagram / chart / flow chart / table / graph / pie chart / bar graph/ line graph / table data/	shows/ illustrates / presents/ gives/ describes/ compares/ shows/ represents / depicts/ provides/ gives data on/ gives information on/ shows data about/ presents information about	the number of …. the comparison of …. the differences …. the proportion of…. the amount of …. information on …. data on ….

VOCABULARY TO SHOW THE CHANGES

Trends	Verb form	Noun Form
Decrease	decline/ fall/ decrease/ plummet/ plunge/ drop/ reduce	a decline/ a fall/ a decrease/ a downward trend/ a downward tendency/ a drop
Increase	go up/ increase/ rise/ rocketed/ climb/ uplift/ soar/ upsurge	an upward trend/ a rise/ a growth/ an increase
Steadiness	unchanged/ remain constant/ level out/ remain steady/ remain the same/ plateau/ remain stable	a stability/ a steadiness/ a plateau/ a static
Gradual decrease	------	a downward tendency/ a downward trend
Gradual Increase	------	an upward tendency/ an upward trend.

VOCABULARY TO REPRESENT COMPARISON IN GRAPHS

Type	Word(s) should be used
Just over	just bigger/ just above/ just across/ just beyond
Just under	just beneath/ just below/ just a little
Similar	nearly/ about/ around/ almost/ approximately/ just about/ very nearly
Much less	well under/ well beneath/ well below
Much more	well beyond/ well above/ well over

VOCABULARY TO WRITE THE CONCLUSION PART

To draw the conclusion

- To conclude

- In conclusion

- On the whole

To Summarize

- In brief

- In short

- To sum up

- In summary

USEFUL TIME EXPRESSIONS

- (In) the period from…...to…….../ between……and [(in) the period from June to August... between June and August...]

- During (during the first three months...)

- In the first/ last three months of the year

- Over the period from…….to……..

- Over the next...for the following... (for the following two months... Over the next six months...)

- Over a ten-year period

- Throughout the 19th century

- From that time on

- After that/ then

USEFUL EXPRESSIONS OF MEASUREMENT

- The amount of (production/ coffee)

- The number of (cars/ unemployed people)

- The quantity of (coffee/ students)

- The percentage/ proportion of (women in workforce)

- The rate of birth growth/ unemployment

Percentage language:

77%	just over three-quarters
77%	approximately three-quarters
49%	just under a half
49%	nearly a half
32%	almost a third
75% - 85%	a very large majority
65% - 75%	a significant proportion
10% - 15%	a minority
5%	a very small number

STRUCTURES FOR DESCRIBING TRENDS

- S + V + Adverb + Figure + Time.

- There + Be + A/An + Adjective + Noun + Figure + In + Noun (+ Time)

- S + Experience/ Witness/ Undergo/ See + A/An + Adjective + Noun + In + Noun

STRUCTURES FOR WRITING INTRODUCTION

1.   The line graph shows trends/ changes in the number/ amount of +
Noun (+ relative clause) + in place + time.

2.   The line graph chart shows Information/ data about how many/ how
much + Noun + V...

OVERVIEW PARAGRAPH

What makes a good overview? Here are a few tips:

• An overview is simply a summary of the main things you can see.

• Putting it at the beginning of your essay, just after the introduction sentence.

• Writing two overview sentences. A one-sentence overview isn't really enough.

• Try not to include specific numbers in the overview. Save the specifics for later paragraphs.

DETAIL PARAGRAPHS

- It's important to include numbers and make some comparisons

- Here is a list of useful words to describe a number, a trend or to make a comparison:

• Describe a number: (verb) stood at, peak in, approximately...

• Describe a trend :

- Things going up: (verb/noun) increase, rise, jump, climb, peak (highest figure)...

- Things going down; (verb) fall, drop, fall, decrease, decline, bottom out (lowest figure)...

- Noun: slump, plunge, fall, decrease...

- Adjective: downward, upward

- Adverb: noticeably = markedly = remarkably < significantly = drastically = radically = considerably

- Slightly = somewhat

- Suddenly = rapidly = dramatically = speedily = sharply

- Steadily = gradually = increasingly

- Approximately = about = around = roughly = more or less

- Respectively

- Such as = namely

TABLES

Tips for tables:

•   Make sure you highlight some key numbers before you start writing. Then, skim and select the biggest number in each category in the table. If the table shows time like years, months, then look for the biggest changes in figures over the time period. Also, you could mention the smallest numbers, but you must ignore the 'middle'.

•   For the summary paragraph, try to make comparisons of the whole categories rather than individual ones in the table. If you are unable to compare whole categories, just compare the biggest and smallest number. One more thing, you should write 2 sentences for the summary.

•   Never describe each category separately in your two 'details' paragraphs. The examiner wants to see you make comparisons. Try to place the numbers you highlighted into 2 groups - one for each paragraph (e.g. the highest numbers and the lowest numbers).

•   Describe/ compare the numbers you highlighted – make sure there are at least 3 numbers included in each paragraph.

•   Highly recommend using the past simple for past years, and "will" or "is expected/predicted to" for future years. If no time is shown, use the present simple is the best choice.

TABLE SAMPLE

Summarize the information by selecting and reporting the main feature and make comparisons where relevant.

You should spend about 20 minutes on this task.

Write at least 150 words

The percentage of school aged boys in two different age groups who participated in 5 different sports in the UK in 2010

sports	boys 6-11	boys 12-16
football	87	78
basketball	35	25
cricket	45	34
rugby	23	21
swimming	19	19

In this same year, the proportion of both age groups in the UK who liked swimming was the same, at 19%. Additionally, the UK saw a similar figure for schoolboys aged 6-11 and 12-16 who played rugby in 2010, at 23% and 21% respectively.

Note: If we describe something as 'similar' we already mean that it is "nearly/almost the same '

Model answer:

The table shows data on the proportion of schoolboys in 2 separate age groups who took part in playing 5 kinds of sports in the UK in 2010.

Overall, the figures for boys between 6 and 11 years old are always higher than those for the older boys, with the notable exception of swimming, which is the same.

While 87% of 6-to 11-year-olds played soccer, the percentage of boys between 12 and 16 was slightly lower, at 78%. Only 25% of the older age group played basketball, compared to 35% of the younger boys. The percentage of younger boys who participated in cricket was 45% and 34% for the older group; a difference of 11%

In this same year, the proportion of both age groups in the UK who liked swimming was the same, at 19%. Additionally, the UK saw a similar figure for schoolboys aged 6-11 and 12-16 who played rugby in 2010, at 23% and 21% respectively.

(168 words)

IELTS EXAMINER COMMENTS

The paraphrase paragraph is band 9 level. It uses your own words and - as a description of the table - it is clear, complete and accurate.

You identified two key features in the summary paragraph. So, this was a good overview.

Your reporting of percentages in your detail paragraphs was accurate and you made constant comparisons between the two sets of figures.

To be honest, the report which you sent me would score band 9 and could be used as a model answer. There are no corrections to make, because the information, grammar and vocabulary are all accurate, many comparisons are made and the organization of the report is superb.

USEFUL VOCABULARY

•   **Data on:** data is information, figures, statistics that can be shown in a table, bar graph or other types of visual representations; "this table shows data on the type of sports that each group of boys played"

•   **Proportion of:** a proportion of something is a part, share, or portion of a whole; the comparative relation between parts; "a large proportion of the residents in megacities must use public transportation"; "a large proportion of the boys played football"

•   **Took part in:** to perform; to play; to be involved in; "he took part in four different shows last year"; "she took part in the first three meetings but missed the final one"; "in both groups, 19% of boys took part in swimming"

•   **Notable exception of:** notable means that it is worthy of noticing or taking something into consideration; remarkable; outstanding; exception means a person or thing that is excluded from a place or a rule; not present; an exception is something that doesn't conform to the general rule or situation; "very important officials were at the meeting with the notable exception of the president" (that means the president wasn't there); "with the notable exception of swimming, a larger percentage of younger boys took part in sports overall".

•   **Participated in:** you participate in something, like a sport, a game, a class, an event, a competition; you take part in it, you perform in it; "my sons participated in a class on computer programming this past week"; "she participated in sports up until she was 15"; "the table shows that more than half the boys in both groups participated in football"

•   **Additionally:** used as a transition word when you want to add more information to the paragraph, followed by a comma; when discussing the information in a table or chart, you can say something about the data and then add something else about the same category; "additionally, the table shows that there was an equal percentage of boys who participated in swimming"; "additionally, early clinical trials have indicated that the drug might also help treat diabetes"

- **Similar figures**: similar means like or almost the same or sharing some features or characteristics; figure meaning the number; "similar figures were found for the incidence of arthritis in this population in two different studies"; "this table shows similar figures for rugby"

- **Respectively:** used to talk about something in precisely the order given; sequentially; "their weights were 80 kg and 100 kg, respectively" always separated by a comma; "the percentage of boys 6-11 and boys 12-16 who played rugby was 23 and 21, respectively."

TABLE SAMPLE 2:

Proportion of household income five European countries spend on food and drink, housing, clothing and entertainment.

	Food and drink	Housing	Clothing	Entertainment
France	25%	31%	7%	13%
Germany	22%	33%	15%	19%
UK	27%	37%	11%	11%
Turkey	36%	20%	12%	10%
Spain	31%	18%	8%	15%

Model answer:

The table gives information about the percentage of income which residents in 5 European nations spend on 4 different items every month.

Overall, in all five countries, citizens spend the highest proportion of their income on food and drink and housing and significantly less on clothing and entertainment.

Of the five countries, Turkish and Spanish households spend the highest percentages of their income on food and drink monthly with 36% and 31%, respectively. However, only 27% of income is spent on this item by UK households, compared to 25% by the French and 22% by the German people. In contrast, people in all other nations tend to spend the highest proportion of their income on housing. In France, Germany and the UK, people spend more than 30% of their income on this item, at 31%, 33% and 37%, respectively. The figures for Turkey are just 20% and for Spain, 18%.

The amounts of money, as a percentage of income, that citizens spend for clothing and entertainment are lower. In France and Spain, people spend only 7% and 8% of their wages on clothing, respectively. The figures for the remaining nations are below 15%. Likewise, the average percentage of income that residents spend on entertainment only ranges from 10% to 19% in these five countries.

IELTS EXAMINER COMMENTS

You managed to include all the key points (such as 'every month') and to use enough of your own words.

I am quite happy with the key features that you chose to report in your summary paragraph. This should convince the examiner that you have a good overview of the information in the table.

The division of your detail paragraphs was completely clear and logical, following the key feature which you had just reported in your summary. Paragraph 3 focused on the two highest categories of household expenditure. You managed to include all the percentages given in the table. You reported all of them accurately and you made useful comparisons throughout the paragraph.

In paragraph 4, you reported on the spending on clothes and entertainment. Here, you selected information and I think that this was well chosen and expressed reasonably clearly.

You correctly used the present simple tense consistently throughout the report. This showed again that you read the task question and studied the table carefully.

USEFUL VOCABULARY

• **The highest proportion of their income:** the largest part or portion (as a percentage) of the money they bring into their household; "The highest portion of their income was spent on housing"

• **Spent significantly less on:** to spend a lot less on something than on something else; we use the preposition on to talk about how you spend your money to buy something; "They spent significantly less on clothing than they did on food."

• **Food and drink:** food would be groceries and drink would be beverages; "The Turks spent quite a lot of their income on food and drink."

• **Compared to:** used to talk about two or more things; "Compared to the Spanish, the Germans spent more money on clothing."

• **In contrast:** used to say something different about another group of variables; "In contrast to the Germans, who spent 15% of their income on clothing, the French spent a mere 7%."

• **Are just:** only; merely; "The figures for how much the French and the Spanish spent on clothing, as a percentage of their income, are just 7% and 8%, respectively."

• **The amounts of money:** the total sum of money; another way to say it so that you don't keep saying the same words; "The amounts of money they spent on food and clothing were not so high."

• **Clothing and entertainment:** refers to the category of money spent on clothes and things like going to the movies; "They spent more than 10% of their income on clothing and entertainment."

• **Spend their wages on:** to spend your income on; wages is what you get paid for your job, also salary; "They don' like to spend so much of their wages on housing."

• **Likewise:** in the same way; at the same time; in a similar way; "According to the information in the table, the Germans appear, likewise, to spend a lesser percentage of their income on clothing."

- **Ranges from:** to talk about a span or space between two different figures: "The amount of money you can make in this business ranges from nothing to millions."

LINE GRAPH

Tips for Line graph

• It would be excellent if you can write 4 paragraphs in your paper – 1 introduction, 1 summary of main points, and 2 detail paragraphs.

• For the summary of main points paragraph, try to look at the "big picture" – see what changes happened to all of the lines from the beginning to the end of the given period of time (i.e. from the first year to the last year). See if any trend that all of the lines follow (e.g. an overall decrease/increase)?

• Don't include numbers in the summary paragraph. You just mention general things like "overall change", "highest" and "lowest", without giving specific numbers.

• Don't ever…ever…never describe each line separately. Make comparisons. The examiner wants to see your comparisons.

• Remember that if the graph shows years, you just select the key years to describe. For example, you just pick the first year and the last year to illustrate. Since you won't have enough time to mention all of them.

• For the 1st detail paragraph among two, you start describing details with a comparison of the lines for the first given year shown on the graph (e.g. In 2005, the number of/the figure for...).

• Highly recommend using the past simple (increased/rose, decreased) for past years, and 'will' or 'is expected/predicted to' for future years.

OUTLINE FOR TASK 1: LINE GRAPHS

INTRODUCTION

- The graph shows trends/ changes in + noun phrases...

- The graph shows (that/ how many/ how much ...)

General Trend:

- It is clearly seen from the graph that...

- There was an upward trend/ a downward trend in...

- S + V + ADV

- S + witness/ see/ experience + a/an + adj + noun (+ figure + time)

BODY

- Description of significant details.

(Regarding X, Similarly/ Likewise, to contrast/ On the other hand/ However,...)

CONCLUSION

- Overall, we can see from the graph that...

- The overall chart shows ...

LINE GRAPH SAMPLE

You should spend about 20 minutes on this task.

The graph below compares changes in the birth rates of China and the USA between 1920 and 2000.

Summarize the information by selecting and reporting the main features, and make comparisons where relevant.

Write at least 150 words.

Birth Rates in China and the USA

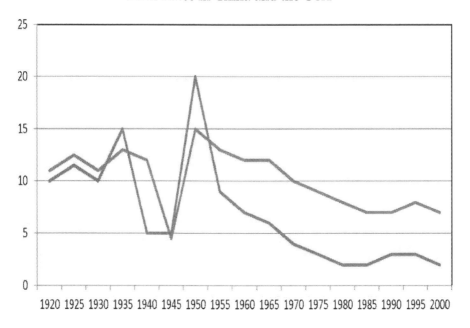

Model answer:

The line graph compares birth rates in China and the US and how these rates changed from 1920 to 2000.

Overall, the birth rates of both nations decreased over the period of 80 years. Although the two trends were similar in terms of a general decline, the birth rate of the USA in most years was higher than that of China.

In the 1920-1935 period, the birth rate in America fluctuated, although it always remained above 10%. However, in the following decade, the American birth rate fell sharply to below 5%. In the 1950s, the figure for the USA increased significantly to exactly 15%, which was its highest point during the 80-year period. Throughout the remainder of the period, there was a gradual decline in the US birth rate, which fell to 7% by the year 2000.

Over the same period, the birth rate in China varied more significantly than in the US. It dropped to 5% from 1940 to 1945 before reaching the highest point of the whole line graph, 20%, in 1950. By contrast, 5 years later, the birth rate in China decreased rapidly by over 10%, falling to approximately 2% in 2000.

(Band 8.0+)

USEFUL VOCABULARY

• **In terms of:** speaking of; used to tell the reader what you are referring to; in this case you are referring to the general decline in the birth rate; with respect to; regarding; "In terms of learning how to speak a foreign language, it is important to listen as much as possible."

• **A general decline:** an overall decrease or lessening in number; "There was a general decline in the amount of junk food people ate over the last decade."

• **Fluctuate:** to change, up and down; "Investors didn't like how the stock market fluctuated last year."

• **Remain above:** to stay higher than, in terms of numbers; we usually say above rather than over when describing a higher number; "The sales numbers for last quarter remained above our previous forecasts."

• **Fall sharply:** to fall means to go down; sharply means all of a sudden and by a lot; "The prices fell sharply due to the higher level of production and fewer buyers in the market."

• **Below:** we use below rather than under in this case; "The graph shows that China's birth rate stayed well below that of the USA from 1955 onward."

• **Throughout the remainder of the period:** throughout means during; the remainder means the rest of; the period refers to the time, the years; "Our sales figures stayed above $10,000 per day throughout the remainder of the period."

• **Gradual decline:** gradual means it takes time, not sudden(ly) or quick; decline means it goes down, a decrease; "There was a gradual decline in the health of their pets once they moved to the city."

• **Varied more significantly than:** to vary means to change; significantly means by an important amount; "The immigration laws varied more significantly in the U.S. than they did in Canada."

- **Dropped to:** to fall to; to go down to a certain level; "The birth rate dropped to more than half by 1955."

- **Decreased rapidly:** to decrease is to go down, to drop, to decline; rapidly means quickly, in a fast way; "The temperature decreased rapidly once they were in the mountains."

- **Falling to:** decreasing to; dropping to; going down to a specific amount; "The stock price hit an all-time low today, falling to $5 per share."

BAR CHART

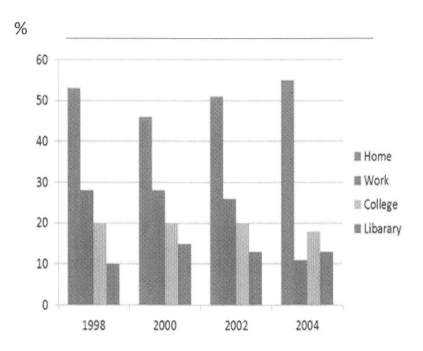

The bar chart illustrates data on the percentage of users connecting to the Internet in 4 types of locations between 1998 and 2004.

Overall, the percentage of people who used the Internet at home and in the library remained relatively constant, while the figures for access at work and college decreased. Also, home was by far the most common place where users accessed the Internet

In 1998, the proportion of users accessing the Internet from home was the highest, at around 54%. By contrast, the rate for those who used it at the library was at the lowest point of exactly 10%. Approximately 27% of users connected to the Internet at work, compared to precisely 20% at college.

The percentage of Internet users gaining access from their houses rose to approximately 55% in 2004, after a decline of about 8% in 2000. On the other hand, the figures for access at work and college decreased to exactly 10% and around 18%, respectively, over the period. Users accessing the Internet at the library increased about 5% from 1998 to 2000 and then dipped slightly in 2002, where it remained steady throughout 2004.

(Band 8.0+)

IELTS EXAMINER COMMENTS

You covered all the requirements of the task, and all the information that you reported was accurate.

You selected information effectively and your report was clear throughout. I noted that you made relevant comparisons between the figures and the trends. There is a lot of information in the chart – it is quite deceptive because at first, it appears that we would be able to report almost everything, but this is not the case.

So, I found that your detail paragraphs were organized logically, enabling trends and differences to be compared.

My combined score for task achievement and coherence/cohesion is 9.

Some repetition is unavoidable in the language used, such as access/ Internet users, and this is quite legitimate in order to present a clear and accurate report. Of course, it is great to use language such as By contrast/ However/ On the other hand..... Because these are very effective words when we want to draw contrasts. You varied your use of percentage/rate/proportion and I noted your good expression 'by far the most common...' I scored 9 again for the lexical resource.

Your grammar was faultless, and I noted how you varied your sentence structures. For example, in paragraph 3, you began one sentence with the percentage: Approximately 27% of users connected to.... The examiner should also notice your correct use of subordinate [adverb and relative clauses] and superlatives. I have to score 9 for grammar.

My overall score is 9, a good band 9 model answer.

USEFUL VOCABULARY

- **Decreased:** went down, declined; "rents decreased from $1,000 per month to $800 per month"

- **By far:** by a long way, by a lot; "he was by far the strongest man in the room"

- **By contrast:** used when you compare two things together and you talk about the differences, the contrast refers to how they are different; you can also say in contrast; "she performed well on her final exams; by contrast, her brother failed his finals"

- **Approximately:** almost, just about, nearly; "they made approximately $5,000 last night at the concert"

- **Precisely:** exactly, the precise number or figure; "they made precisely $6.00 per sale"

- **Gaining access:** to be able to get access to something after not having access to it; "more and more people are gaining access to the Internet"

- **Rise:** went up, increased; "temperatures rose yesterday by 10 degrees"

- **A decline of:** a decrease of; going down; "there was a decline in overall stock prices yesterday"

- **On the other hand:** used to say something different about something; usually used to say the opposite and give a reason; "on the one hand, she is quite intelligent and open minded; on the other hand, she doesn't always do well on her exams and can be quick to judge people"

- **Over the period:** to describe the duration of time during a period of time; "over the period of a month, she has learned so much Spanish"

- **Dipped slightly:** to dip means to go down or to decline; slightly means by a little; "the price of apples dipped slightly last month:

- **Remained steady throughout:** to stay about the same during a time period; "the cost of gas remained steady throughout the summer months"

•   **Illustrates data on:** to illustrate means to show, to demonstrate; data (or data) includes information, figures, statistics, numbers, percentages, etc…when you write "data on" it means that you will show specific information about a topic, some research, numbers, etc; "this table illustrates data on the ages of residents in our town"

•   **Locations:** areas, spaces, where something is located; "our store has many locations throughout town"

•   **Remained relatively constant:** to remain means to stay; relatively means related to other things, in relation to; mostly; constant means the same; to remain relatively constant means to stay mostly the same as before; "home prices remained relatively constant throughout the year"

PIE CHART

The graphs below show a comparison of the expenses in the UK and the US.

Summarise the information by selecting and reporting the main features, and make comparisons where relevant.

Expenses in the UK   Expenses in the US

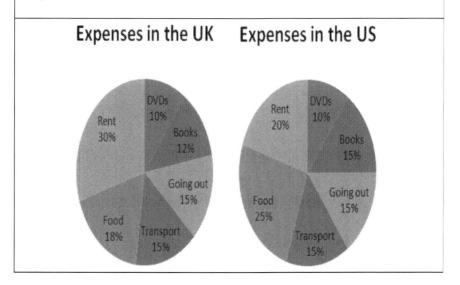

Model answer:

The pie charts compare the UK and the US in terms of different categories of expenditures.

Overall, spending on rent and food accounts for the largest proportions of expenses in both the UK and the US. In addition, people in both countries spend a similar percentage of their budget on the remaining four categories.

The percentage of spending on DVDs is exactly the same in both nations, 10%. Likewise, people in the UK and America spend 15% of their expenditures on transport. People in the UK and the US both spend 15% of total expenses on going out.

In the UK, the largest expenditure is for rent, at 30%, while the figure for the US is just 20%. In terms of food, the figure for the US is slightly more than that of the UK, at 25% and 18%, respectively. Finally, the Americans spend 3% more on books than their counterparts in the UK.

(154 words)

IELTS EXAMINER COMMENTS

The first paraphrase paragraph is clear, concise and uses enough of your own words.

You identified two key features of the charts in your summary paragraph. I can't improve on this overview – I choose the same two features.

You organized your detail paragraphs sensibly and this division of paragraphs followed what you had written in your summary paragraph.   All the information is accurately reported in paragraphs 3 and 4.   You also made comparisons between the spending patterns in the two countries as well as between the different categories of spending.

The report, therefore, is accurate and complete.   It is also well organised with an excellent overview.   I, therefore, scored 9 for task achievement and coherence/cohesion.   In terms of vocabulary, spending is a useful and exact synonym for expenditure. It is impossible to avoid repetition of these words – we have to use them several times to make the report clear.

You have tried to vary your sentence structures. I scored 8.5 combined for grammar and lexical resource and this gives an overall score of 8.5.

USEFUL VOCABULARY

• **Different categories of:** various types of things; different is used when things are not the same; a category is used to divide up things into different sorts or types of things; "there were quite a few different categories of evidence used in the court case"

• **Spending on:** you spend money on something when you pay for that thing; "they have been spending a lot of money on clothing lately"

• **Accounts for:** to be the reason for something; "high crime in the neighborhood accounts for the low home prices"

• **Similar percentage of:** similar means to be almost the same or nearly the same as something else; percentage of something means the portion or part of out of the whole, out of 100 percent; "they each own a similar percentage of stocks in the business"

• **Remaining categories:** remaining means what is left over; the rest; regarding the pie chart, it means the categories that haven't been talked about yet; "they spent about the same in the remaining four categories"; "she didn't like any of the remaining four topics, so she decided to leave the workshop early"

• **Likewise:** used to explain when something is done the same way or looks the same or gives the same or similar information; in the same vein; at the same time; in the same manner; too; also; the same as; in the pie chart it means that both countries spend the same amount on DVDs and also on transport; "they both spend the same on DVDs. Likewise, they each spend 15% on transport."

• **Slightly more than:** a little bit more than something else; "she is slightly heavier than her brother"; "she will have to pay slightly more than she wanted"; in the pie chart, it expresses that one country spends a little bit more money in one category than another

IELTS WRITING TASK 1 - MIXED TYPE (LINE AND BAR CHART)

STRUCTURE

INTRODUCTION:

Write the opening sentence as usual by paraphrasing (rewrite the question of the assignment by your own words). With Task 1 mixed type graph questions, it will be easier if you give out 2 examples eg "The first chart illustrates ... The second chart shows ..."

OVERVIEW:

Write 1-2 sentences that describe the main features, key features. Often in each chart, find one main feature to describe.

BODY 1: Describe the main features of the chart 1

BODY 2: Describe the main features of the chart 2. Note that simply describes each chart individually. No need to have a comparison or connection between Chart 1 and Chart 2.

Task 1: The graph and chart give information and forecast about the vehicle and C02 emission in England and Wales between 2000 and 2020

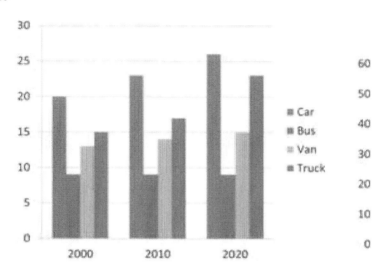

Task 1 plan:

Introduction: paraphrase task heading

Summary paragraph - 2 key features: **[1]** bar chart: increasing C02 emissions - cars, vans, and trucks **[2]** line graph: increase in the number of road vehicles

Paragraph 3: bar chart details: compare C02 emissions in 2000 from cars, vans and trucks. Contrast with low figure for buses. Compare predicted 2020 emissions from cars, vans and trucks. Contrast again with low figure for buses.

Paragraph 4: give a number of road vehicles in 2000 and note trend 2000-2015. Give 2015 figure. Give projected figure for 2020.

Model answer:

The bar chart compares the amount of CO2 emissions produced by four types of vehicles. The line graph shows the number of vehicles. Both diagrams refer to England and Wales for the period 2000 to 2020.

Overall, the chart indicates a rise in the emission of CO_2 from cars, vans and trucks between these years. The graph shows that the number of vehicles on the road is expected to continue to increase sharply.

In 2000, CO_2 emissions from cars were the highest figure at 20 tons. The emissions from trucks and vans were similar, at 15 and 13 tons respectively, whereas the emissions from buses totalled just 9 tons. By 2020, a rise in car emissions to over 25 tons of CO_2 is forecast, with a smaller rise in emissions from trucks and vans. It is predicted that trucks will produce about 23 tons and vans will emit 15 tons. In contrast, the figure for CO_2 emissions from buses will continue to be the lowest amount, remaining stable at 9 tons.

The number of road vehicles was 20 million in 2000. This increased rapidly to 50 million by 2015 and is expected to increase to 55 million by 2020.

IELTS EXAMINER COMMENTS

Task achievement: There was quite a lot of information contained in these two diagrams. I think that you did a good job of selecting key details and reporting them clearly, focusing on the first and final years [2000 and 2020]. You also made many relevant comparisons throughout the report. All the figures were reported accurately.

In the summary paragraph, you chose significant details. You expressed concern about the word count, although - as we know - you will certainly not lose marks for writing this number of words. One way to reduce the word count in this report could be to mention one significant feature only from each diagram There is nothing that I would add to this report, so I consider that it presents a 'fully developed response ' and score band 9 for this section.

Coherence and cohesion: There is a clear and planned structure. The information is sequenced logically, moving the reader consistently from the year 2000 to the year 2020, with your description of the trends linking these start points and end points effectively and clearly.

There was enough variety in your sentence structures, so don't worry about synonyms for key words in diagrams in task 1. Think about using 'While/ Whereas' in task 1 - they are useful adverb clauses to indicate contrast.

Lexical resource: You used a range of vocabulary correctly when referring to future predictions of the number of road vehicles. See Simon's blog of January 19, 2012.

Grammatical range and accuracy:

I noted your correct grammar for comparisons and superlative forms.

USEFUL VOCABULARY

- **Emissions:** [noun] gases and very small particles sent out into the air.

Example: in big cities, the emissions from vehicles damage the quality of the air.

- **Diagram:** [noun] any kind of simple drawing, used to explain something.

Example: in the IELTS exam, we may have to report on any of these diagrams: pie charts, bar charts, line graphs, processes, flow charts of life cycles.

- **Sharply:** [adverb] suddenly and by a large amount.

Example: following the economic crisis in the USA, the value of the American dollar fell sharply over a period of a few days.

- **Respectively**: [adverb] in the same order as the things already mentioned.

Example: john and peter are aged 17 and 19 respectively.

- **Total:** [verb] reach a particular total.

Example: last year, imports from china totalled $10 billion.

- **Forecast:** [verb] say what you think will happen in the future, based on the information that you have now. [grammar note: there are 2 correct past participles: forecast/forecasted].

Example: the storm presently causing a lot of damage in Thailand is forecast to arrive in Malaysia tomorrow.

- **Emit:** [verb] send out something, like gases for example.

Example: when the volcano exploded, it emitted clouds of gases and smoke into the air.

- **Stable:** [adjective] not moving or changing, remaining constant.

Example: the chart shows that the emissions of c02 from buses remained stable between 2000 and 2010.

PROCESS DIAGRAM

Tips for process diagram

Process diagrams show how something is done or made. They always show steps/stages. Here's some advice about how to describe them:

•   Try to write 4 paragraphs - introduction, a summary of main points, 2 detail paragraphs.

•   Write the introduction by paraphrasing the question (rewrite it by changing some of the words).

•   For your summary, first, say how many steps there are in the process. Then say where/how the process begins and ends (look at the first and last stages).

•   In paragraphs 3 and 4, describe the process step by step. Include the first and last steps that you mentioned in the summary, but try to describe them in more detail or in a different way.

•   Mention every stage in the process.

•   Use 'sequencing' language e.g. at the first/ second/ following/ final stage of the process, next, after that, then, finally etc.

•   Highly recommend using the present simple tense because times (e.g. past dates) are not usually given.

•   It's usually a good idea to use the passive e.g. 'At the final stage, the product is delivered to shops' (because we don't need to know who delivered the product).

•   Use the active to describe a natural process and the passive to describe a man-made process.

PROCESS WRITING STRUCTURE

INTRODUCTION

1.   The chart/diagram (shows/describes/illustrates) how + clause

E.g. the diagram shows how fresh apple is canned

2.   The chart/ diagram (shows/describe/illustrates) + noun

E.g. The figure illustrates the process used by the Australian Bureau of Meteorology to forecast the weather.

3.   The chart/diagram (provides/gives) information about...

E.g. The diagram provides information about the involved stages in the lives of silkworms and the process of silk cloth production

OVERVIEW:

•   There are ....main stages (steps) in the process/in the process of producing...,beginning with.. .and ending with.

•   The process (of producing.) includes.. .main stages (steps)., beginning with,…. and ending with.

BODY:

ORDERING LANGUAGES

First Stage

•   First of all/ First/ Firstly

•   The first stage is when + noun + verb

•   The first step/phase/stage is/involves...

•   At the beginning of...

•   To begin with,

•   The process commences with

Middle Stages

• Secondly/ Thirdly/ Subsequently /Subsequent To That/ Then/ Next/ After That/ Following On/ From This/ Following That

• The next step is when + noun + verb

• The step after this + verb

Use the following conjunctions to make more complex sentences:

• Once/As Soon As/ When/ Immediately

• Before + clause or gerund

• After + clause or gerund

• Once A has finished, B is able to start

• After this stage is complete,

Last Stage

• At the end of...

• Finally,

• The final stage/ step/ phase is

• Once the final stage has been completed,

Expressing Purpose

• X is done (so as) to produce Y.

• X is done in other that Y can be produced.

• so that,

Expressing cause and effect

• Because Of/ Due To/ Owing To + Noun

• Since/ As/ Because + Clause

- X Results From Y

- Consequently/ As A Result/ Therefore + Clause

- This Results In + Noun

- X Results In Y

- X Happens, Which Results Y

- X Happens, With The Result That Y Happens

- So + Clause /So + Adj/Adv + That + Clause

PROCESS SAMPLE

The diagram illustrates the process that is used to manufacture bricks for the building industry.

Summarize the information by selecting and reporting the main features and make comparisons where relevant.

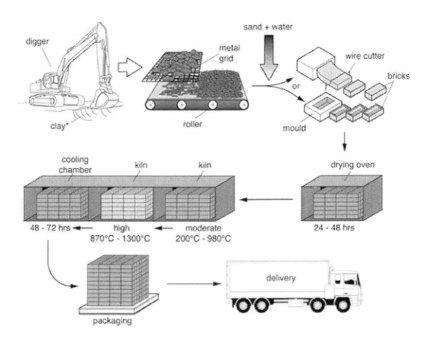

Model answer:

The flow chart shows how bricks are produced for, and delivered to the building industry

Overall, there are 7 stages in the whole brick producing process, beginning with clay excavation and ending with the delivery of the bricks to the customers.

Firstly, clay is dug up by using a big digger. To get rid of the oversized pieces, clay is placed on a metal grid and small pieces drop onto a large roller. At the next stage, sand and water are added to the clay. After the bricks are shaped by using a wire cutter or a mould, they are moved to a drying oven for 24 to 48 hours.

Those bricks are then fired in a special kiln at a moderate temperature (200c - 980c) at the fourth step. Afterwards, they continue to be heated for the second time at a higher temperature (870c - 1300c) in another kiln. Before being packaged at the sixth stage, the bricks are treated in a cooling chamber for 48 to 72 hours. The entire brick producing process concludes after the bricks are delivered to customers.

IELTS EXAMINER COMMENTS

This is without any doubt a band 9 report. It is just as good as the model answer. The report is factually correct and you include everything shown in the diagram. Well done on such a thorough and well-written report!

+ Task response:

The first sentence is a good paraphrase. It is clear, concise and it uses enough of your own words. The summary paragraph which follows provides a clear overview, using exactly the right technique (stating the number of steps and referring specifically to the first and last stages).

+ Coherence and cohesion

You divided your detailed paragraphs sensibly and logically - it was easy for the reader to follow each stage. You varied your language to begin your description of each new stage in the process: Firstly/ At the next stage/ When/ at the fourth step/ Afterwards/ Before being packaged at the sixth stage

+ Lexical resource:

I was really impressed by your range of vocabulary, and I noted your excellent use of phrasal verbs: dug up/get rid of. To avoid confusion, you correctly used the same words as in the diagram to refer to each stage.

+ Grammar:

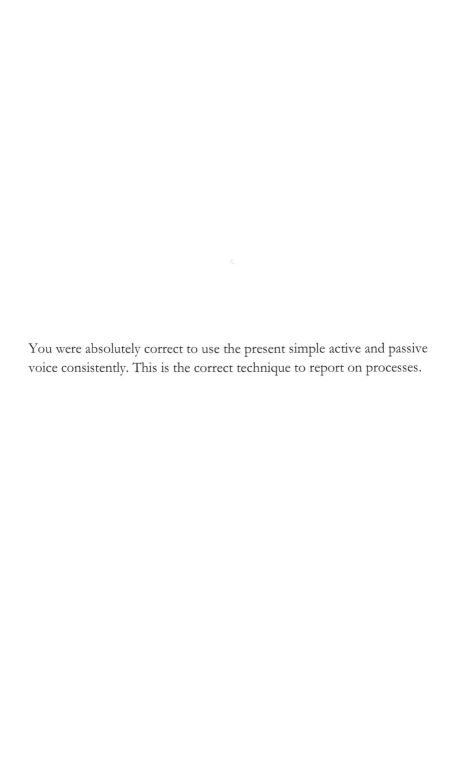

You were absolutely correct to use the present simple active and passive voice consistently. This is the correct technique to report on processes.

USEFUL VOCABULARIES FOR WRITING PROCESSES

• **Clay:** clay is a type of earth which is very heavy, unlike sand which is relatively light

• **Brick:** a brick is a rectangular object made by heating clay until it becomes solid. It is used in many countries to construct houses or other buildings.

• **Digger:** the machine shown in the diagram is often referred to [at least in the UK] as a JCB. Its function is to 'dig' or to make a hole in the ground.

• **Excavation:** although there are two similar verbs - 'dig' and 'excavate', the noun 'excavation' is commonly used in the construction industry. It suggests something on a large scale where we make a big hole in the ground, as in the excavation of clay for example.

• **Dug up:** note the irregular past simple tense/and past participle of the verb 'dig'. Here the phrasal verb 'dig up' is used to mean an activity when we make a hole in the ground with a machine.

• **Cutter:** in the same way as a 'digger' is something which digs, a 'cutter' is something which cuts. In this case, the cutter is made or 'wire' or thin metal as shown in the diagram.

• **Mould:** a mould is an object which is used to form a shape. In this case, the sand and water mixture is placed in a mould to make the shape of a brick.

• **Fire:** the verb 'fire' has several meanings. Here, it refers to the action of heating an object made from clay.

• **Kiln:** a kiln is similar to an oven, but it has a different function. An oven is used for cooking or heating food - usually in the home. A kiln - like the one in the diagram - is usually used in industrial processes for making some material very hard. It can be used in different processes at really high temperatures for heating things, to make iron for example.

• **Chamber:** the process in the diagram shows that the bricks are very hot when they go into this closed space or chamber. They undergo 'cooling' - they become less and less hot.

MAP

The maps below show how the town of Harborne changes from 1936 to 2007.

Summarize the information by selecting and reporting the main features, and make comparisons where relevant.

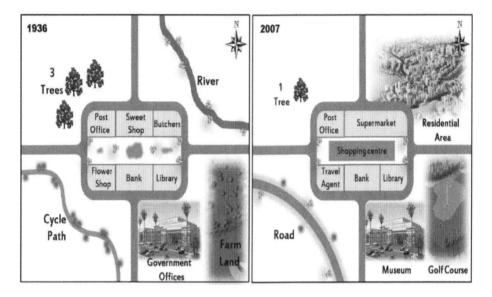

The maps illustrate the transformation of a town called Harborne between 1936 and 2007.

Overall, the town became more developed, cutting out some of the natural beauty while extending the residential area and providing more options for shopping and leisure activities

From 1936 to 2007, the area around the river was developed into a residential area in the northeastern part of the city. The number of trees located in the northwest dropped significantly in the 71 year period.

In the center of the town, they built a new shopping centre and the post office, bank and library remained. The sweet shop and butchers were replaced with a supermarket. Across from the post office, a travel agency was built right on the site where the flower shop used to be. The bike path in the southwest was redesigned as a road. In the southeast, the government offices were converted into a museum, and the adjacent farmland was turned into a golf course.

IELTS EXAMINER COMMENTS

+Task achievement: 8.5

This script is just right length for Task 1. Although not essential, you could include a very brief conclusion just to 'round off' the answer.

Your introduction paraphrases the question well and you give a very clear overview of the changes which have taken place. Your answer focuses on all changes.

+ Cohesion and coherence: 9.0

There is a clear sense of progression and the writing is logically organized. You use linkers well and sentences are well constructed.

+ Lexical resource: 8.5

You use a wide range of vocabulary for describing the maps and the changes. Meaning is clear. + Grammatical range and accuracy 8.5

I'm being very conservative; some examiners would give a 9

This answer is a clear 8.5. Again the final score would depend on whether you get a tough examiner or an easy one. Well done!

USEFUL VOCABULARY

• **Transformation of:** a transformation is when something changes over time; "the transformation of the forest to a residential area caused the deaths of many animals"

• **Overall:** covering or including everything; "the overall total was $150,000 for the month"

• **Cutting out:** to get rid of; to eliminate; "they were cutting out all unnecessary expenditures from the budget"

• **Natural beauty:** the beauty of nature, of outdoor areas, like trees, lakes, rivers, mountains; "the natural beauty of California is very well known"

• **Extending:** to extend means to increase the length, size or duration of something; "they are extending the building to provide more space for new offices"

• **Providing more options for:** to provide for means to offer or to give; more options means more choices; "the company is providing more options for salary increases to their top-performing employees"

• **Leisure activities:** things that are fun to do; fun, recreational activities; not work activities, things you do in your free time; "her favorite leisure activities include reading, swimming, and hiking"

• **To be developed into something:** to take something as it is and create something new in that space; to create; "that part of town was developed into an industrial zone for factories"

• **Dropped significantly:** to drop means to go down, to decline, to decrease; significantly means by a lot, by an important amount: "third quarter sales dropped significantly and the boss was upset"

• **To be replaced with:** to change one thing out for something else; "they replaced the president of the company with a new guy from Taiwan"

- **Built right on the site:** to build something on the exact spot, space or area; "the school was built right on the site where a cemetery used to be"

- **Used to be:** to describe something in the past or something was in the past; "he used to be an accountant, but now he is a stockbroker"; "this town used to be small, but now it is a huge city"

- **Redesigned as:** to change something to be a different way; to make a new design for something; "the old city hall was redesigned as the new office buildings for apple"

- **Converted into:** to change something from one state into another; "the house was converted into a workshop for artists"; "the backyard grass area was converted into a tennis court"

- **Adjacent:** right next to; alongside; "he works in the adjacent office building to mine"

- **Turned into:** it means the same as to convert into; to change from one thing into another; "after four years of being a dance studio, the building was turned into a theater"

MAP LANGUAGE

- In the northwest corner/area of the city

- To the south of the river

- The school was located/situated in the northwest corner of the city

- There was an airport to the south of the lake.

- The school was demolished/knocked down

- All the trees were cut down/chopped down.

- The airport disappeared

- Skyscrapers were built/constructed/erected.

- A park appeared.

- There was a construction of a new hospital.

- The airport was demolished to make way for a new hospital.

- All the trees were replaced by a stadium.

- A stadium was built and replaced all the trees.

- The car park near the river was expanded/widened/extended.

- The school became bigger.

- The railway was lengthened.

- The school was narrowed.

- The car park became smaller.

- The railway was shortened.

- The stadium was moved/relocated to the north.

- The airport still remained/existed.

IELTS WRITING TASK 2

In Academic IELTS writing Task 2, all candidates are required to formulate and develop a position in relation to a given prompt in the form of a question or statement. Ideas should be supported by evidence, and examples may be drawn from the candidates' own experience. Responses must be at least 250 words in length (300 words suggested maximum), 2/3 of your total writing score.

Make sure that you must spend maximum 40 minutes on your essay writing.

Task 2 Band Scores and Marking Criteria

The IELTS examiner will mark you on:

•   Task Achievement (25%)

•   Coherence and Cohesion (25%)

•   Lexical Resource (25%)

•   Grammatical Range and Accuracy (25%)

The examiner will give you a band score for each individual criterion above and then your final score for writing task 1 is the average of the 4.

1. Task AchievementTask Response:

• How well you answer all parts of the task

• You must focus on key points and support every point with evidence.

• Meet the required words count (at least 250 words)

2. Coherence and Cohesion:

• How well-organized your writing is, how well it flows from beginning to end

• Paragraphing and correctly use of words like "however" and "in addition" are essential. Your ideas must be clear and there should be a logical progression from beginning to end.

• You can create a well-organized response for your writing by using linking words or discourse markers as below:

- Introduction: nowadays, in recent times, generally speaking

- For example: one example of this, for instance, such as

- And: moreover, furthermore, in addition, additionally

- Contrast: but, in contrast, despite, yet, however, on the other hand, nevertheless

- Purpose: to, so as to, in order to, in order that, so that.

- Reason: because, due to, since, as, owing to

- Result: therefore, as a result, consequently, in consequence.

3. Lexical Resource (vocabulary)

• How varied, accurate and appropriate your use of vocabulary is (don't repeat the words, bring academic vocabularies in your writing by using adjectives and adverbs)

• Your spelling must be correct (minimize errors in spelling and word formation). Demonstrating the ability to paraphrase and use high-level vocab correctly is important.

4. Grammatical Range and Accuracy

• How varied, accurate and appropriate your use of grammar is

• Using a wide range of sentence structures will help your writing more academically (using complex sentences with both dependent and independent clauses). Of course, you will not get a high score if you make basic grammar errors (e.g. Verb endings, plurals, etc.). Have a control of using punctuation (commas, periods), understand when and how to use it correctly.

DIFFERENT TYPES OF IELTS ACADEMIC TASK 2 WRITING TASKS

IELTS Academic Task 2 writing usually falls into two types of question: **DISCUSSION** and **ARGUMENT (OPINION)**

Type 1: DISCUSSION

You consider different points of view

1.   Discuss the advantages and disadvantages.

2.   What are the benefits and drawbacks?

3.   Discuss both views

DISCUSSION TEMPLATE

INTRODUCTION

+ Paraphrase the topic sentence of the task question

+ While there are benefits to ...., there are also good reasons why it might be beneficial to. Many people suppose that ...., whereas others believe (that)...

BODY

+ On the one hand,.......is attractive for several reasons......is beneficial in some ways

+ On the other hand, there are a variety of reasons why ...

CONCLUSION

In conclusion, it seems evident that ....(both views)....have their own unique advantages.

Type 2: ARGUMENT (OPINION)

When you argue, you are trying to persuade the other person to agree with your point of view.

1. Do you agree or disagree?

2. To what extent do you agree or disagree?

3. Is this a positive or negative development?

ARGUMENT (OPINION) ESSAY SAMPLE

When choosing a job, the salary is the most important consideration. To what extent do you agree or disagree?

ESSAY STRUCTURE:

Introduction

+ Paraphrase the keywords of the topic

+ Answer the question part of the task (note: make your opinion clear)

Body 1: discuss why a high salary is important when choosing a job

+ having a good standard of living

+ motivation

Body 2: two other factors which you consider to be extremely important

+ job satisfaction

+ the contribution that the work may make towards society

Conclusion

+ Paraphrase what you wrote in your introduction

Model essay:

It is true that some job seekers select their career based on salary level. While I accept that this may suit many people, I believe that others base their job choice on more important considerations rather than salary alone.

On the one hand, there are a variety of reasons why people should choose a high-paying job. One reason is that a wage plays an integral part in guaranteeing an acceptable standard of living. Being offered a high salary allows employees to meet their basic needs, buy a comfortable house and perhaps even go on luxury holidays. Furthermore, one of the best motivations is a competitive salary. For example, the head of a company may offer a pay rise to a new employee who is able to achieve a sales target during the year. This rewarding perk will encourage the new sales staff to try hard and enhance the level of job performance.

On the other hand, job seekers have different reasons apart from salary to choose a job. Firstly, job satisfaction is extremely important when people choose their career. If a person adores the outdoor life, he will not be happy being a stockbroker or a financier, no matter that the salaries for both jobs are extremely high. Secondly, contributing to the community is another reason to consider a job. This could bring about a much more civilized society. For instance, Mr. John an Australian man, who has lived in Canada for about 20 years, has constructed 6 schools and other facilities for disabled children instead of working for the Australia Embassy.

In conclusion, it is certainly true that money can be an important factor for many people when choosing prospective employment, but this is by no means the key consideration for everybody in making a career decision.

(297 words)

IELTS EXAMINER COMMENTS

+ Task response:

This was an excellent essay. All the good techniques of task response are here: the task asked for your opinion and you stated this consistently in the introduction and throughout the essay

+ Coherence and cohesion

The examiner is looking for evidence of good planning and organization of your ideas and you provided lots of evidence. You did not try to discuss too many ideas, and this allowed you to discuss each one fully and to use examples. Your paragraph structure was logical and your topic sentences indicated the central idea in each paragraph. Finally, you linked sentences using appropriate and varied expressions, including Firstly/Secondly in paragraph 3. I noted your intelligent use of This as one of the effective linking techniques in this essay.

+ Lexical resource:

There was certainly a sufficient range of vocabulary, accurately used, to express all your ideas clearly.

+ Grammar:

The range of grammar should certainly satisfy the examiner. I found examples of a (first) conditional sentence, a (zero) conditional sentence, relative and adverb clauses and a range of verb tenses. I was also pleased to notice a variety of sentence structures.

USEFUL VOCABULARY

- **To suit somebody** = to be useful or convenient for somebody. The idea here is that a job with a high salary is the most important factor for many people

- **To play an integral part in** = to be an essential part of something.

So, here, a wage is an essential part of achieving a good standard of living

- **A pay rise** = the popular term used for an increase in salary

- **A perk** = something that you receive in addition to your normal salary as an incentive or reward.

- **A stockbroker** = a person who buys and sells shares in companies for other people

- **A financier** = a person who lends large amounts of money to businesses

- **A civilized society** = a society that has laws and customs that are fair and morally acceptable

- **Disabled children** = children who are unable to use part of their body completely or easily because of an injury, an illness or some other physical or mental condition

- **Prospective employment** = employment which is expected to be undertaken soon

PARTLY AGREE/ DISAGREE TEMPLATE

1.   **Introduction**

+ Paraphrase the topic sentence of the task question

+ While I accept that this may suit many people, I believe that …../While I disagree with the idea of….., I do believe that…..

2.   **Body 1:** On the one hand,…

3.   **Body 2:** On the other hand,…

4.   **Conclusion**

In conclusion, it is certainly true that…., but this is by no means …..

TOTALLY AGREE/ DISAGREE TEMPLATE

1.   INTRODUCTION

+ Paraphrase the topic sentence of the task question

+ I do not agree with the idea of …/I do not agree that …/I completely disagree/ agree with this idea.

2.   BODY 1: There are some reasons/a variety of reasons why…..

3.   BODY 2: Apart from the practical benefits/disadvantages expressed above, I believe that…..

4.   CONCLUSION

In conclusion, I believe that…

ADVICE

In the real IELTS academic exam, you should analyze the task carefully, make sure you understand exactly which type of task you need to write before you start writing. Ask yourself the questions: "is this a DISCUSSION or an ARGUMENTATIVE task? Is the task asking me to give my personal viewpoint, or is it asking me to think of some ideas on a topic? Which type of OPINION or IDEAS task is it? Then you should spend a few minutes outlining your essay with some simple notes.

OUTLINE FOR ADVANTAGE - DISADVANTAGE ESSAYS

INTRODUCTION

Introduce the topic | Paraphrase the topic question in your own words | | Tell the reader your plan.

• Nowadays ...These days ... / It cannot be denied that... (Children watching TV) is becoming more and more popular all over the world.

• For many people, the chance to ... (mention one general benefit). However, there are both pros and cons to doing this.

• In this essay, I will discuss some of the reasons why (topic - children's watching TV) is so popular, and some of the challenges to be overcome.

• In this essay, I will explore the pros and cons of (topic - working from home) and try to draw some conclusions.

BODY (2 PARAGRAPHS)

Paragraph 1: List two/ three advantages + explanations/ examples

• Let's start by looking at the advantages of (televisions on children).

• One of the main positives of (televisions) is that ...By this I mean, .../ For example, ...

• Another benefit/ plus of televisions is that... That is to say, .../For instance, ...

• Moreover,...Furthermore,.../In addition,...

Paragraph 2: List two/ three disadvantages + explanations/ examples

• On the other hand..... turning to the other side of the argument..... apart from the advantages...(televisions) also bring about many disadvantages (to children). // On the other hand, we cannot deny the negative effects of (television).

- One of the biggest disadvantages of (watching television) is that ... What I mean by this is that, .../ A good example would be that...

- Another major drawback is that ...In other words, .../ For example, ...

CONCLUSION:

A general, one-sentence summary of the topic + a focused summary of the main points (avoiding repetition of vocabulary) + State your overall opinion.

- All in all/ all things considered/ in conclusion/ to sum up,…(+ reword the topic)…... there are clearly both positives and negatives to + V_ing (i.e. spending an extended period of time overseas)

a)   You need to weigh up the pros of... (+ summarize the benefits), and the cons of... (summarize the drawbacks), (i.e. You need to weigh up the pros of the better lifestyle, weather and so on. and the cons of culture shock and language barrier.)

b)   Summarize the drawbacks and benefits of the issue, using WHILE/ HOWEVER, (i.e. While going abroad can be a great experience and lead to a better lifestyle, for many people, there are too many differences to cope with.)

- In my opinion/ In my view/ As I see it/ Personally, I believe that the benefits eventually outweigh /far exceed any negatives.

USEFUL LANGUAGE TO TALK ABOUT PROS & CONS

- Nouns: benefits/ advantages/ problems/ disadvantages/ drawbacks.

- Verbs: help/ allow/ reduce/ make/ bring/ offer/ have/ limit

- Adjectives: advantageous/ beneficial/ useful/ worthless/ invaluable/ difficult/ helpful/ convenient.

- Linkers: nevertheless/ however/ despite/ in spite of/ although/ but.

ADVANTAGES AND DISADVANTAGES STRUCTURE

INTRODUCTION

1.   Give Background

2.   Introduce the Issue

3.   Paraphrase Advantages/ Disadvantages

BODY PARAGRAPH #1 (2-3 Advantages)

1.   Topic Sentence

2.   Advantages

3.   Example/ Purpose/ Result

BODY PARAGRAPH #2 (2-3 Disadvantages)

1.   Topic Sentence

2.   Disadvantage

3.   Example/ Purpose/ Result

CONCLUSION

1.   Analyse Advantages/ Disadvantages

2.   Final Opinion

OUTLINE FOR DISCUSSION ESSAY

INTRODUCTION

Introduce the topic & identify and state in your own words the two opinions given in the question.

• There is no doubt that/ It cannot be denied that ... (topic introduction)....+ Another extra support sentence - Optional

• The issue of (educating children) remains controversial.

• The issue of whether (introducing the topic) has been debated widely.

- Some people think that (+ VIEW 1), while/whilst others argue that (+ VIEW2).

- In this essay, I will look at both sides of the argument and give my opinion.

BODY (2 PARAGRAPHS)

Discuss both views + reasons/examples

Paragraph 1:

Discuss VIEW 1 + reasons/explanations/ examples

On the one hand, some people are of the opinion that... (+ paraphrasing VIEW 1)

• The first reason is that ... (+ reason 1). For example ...In other words,...

• Another reason is that... (+ reason 2). For Instance ...In fact,...

• Moreover/ Furthermore/ In addition,...

Paragraph 2:

HOWEVER, (discussing the disadvantages of view 1 with reasons/

examples - optional, in case of 2 contrasting views)

CONCLUSION:

Clearly, state your own opinion & which view you support.

- All things considered, ...// In conclusion, ...// To sum up,...

- I feel that... (state your own view). Moreover, I believe that...

SAMPLE

You should spend about 40 minutes on this task

Write about the following topic.

Some people say material possessions are very useful in bringing us happiness, others argue that they are useless in terms of providing happiness. Discuss both views and give your own opinion and reasons.

Give reasons for your answer and include any relevant examples from your own knowledge or experience.

Write at least 250 words.

Model essay:

It cannot be denied that the pursuit of happiness is an everlasting human endeavor in all societies. However, happiness is probably the most elusive thing in the world and when defining it, people would hold widely different views. Some people are of the opinion that they feel happy when they can earn a lot of money and possess expensive and modern belongings, whilst others argue that happiness cannot be bought by ordinary materials or money. In my opinion, although the definitions of happiness may vary, they can fall into two broad categories, which will be discussed below.

On the one hand, some people think they can obtain happiness through acquisition. In fact, their lives are an incessant course of possessing something, whether it is money, fame, authority or social status. A typical example is reflected in the activities of a shrewd businessman, who is in the habit of rushing through life, being on the go from morning till night, motivated by anything that sounds profitable or lucrative. However, the sad thing is that only a few of them can become millionaires after years of striving. A more brutal truth is that many rich people are so obsessed with possessing and retaining their money that it I hard for them to relax and enjoy themselves. Little wonder that some big shots committee suicide because they longed for happiness in another world.

On the other hand, there are some people in the world who achieve happiness through helping others and contributing to the whole society. They are more often ordinary citizens who understand that true happiness comes from giving rather than taking. By devoting themselves to the cause of helping the poor and the disable, they feel an inner bliss that accompanies them at every stumbling block in the way because they are convinced that giving a helping hand to others is a spiritually rewarding act. For instance, we all have the experience of feeling fulfilled and gratified when we have successfully solved a knotty problem for others. It is this kind of charity and generosity that makes our lives rich, meaningful and happy.

To conclude, it seems to me that only through contribution, rather than acquisition, can people actually find themselves immersed in a feeling of happiness. In other words, happiness lies not in anything we possess, but in the act and attitude of helping others

OUTLINE FOR PROBLEM - SOLUTION ESSAYS

INTRODUCTION

Introduce the topic Paraphrase the topic question in your own words
Tell the reader your plan

• Nowadays ...These days ...It cannot be denied that... (Children watching TV is becoming more and more popular all over the world)..., negatively affecting on someone/something.

• The problem is getting worse and worse in my country - China, and it is important to take steps to improve the situation.

• This essay will look at the reasons for this and propose some solutions.

Useful phrases for writing Introduction

• It is clear that (watching TV) is becoming more popular.

• It has become less common for people to ...

• People often consider...

• The problem is becoming worse and worse

• There is no doubt that...

• Most people say...

• It has become evident that...

Time expressions

• Over the past few years + present perfect

• In the last decade + present perfect Present continuous + all the time Recently + present perfect

• Nowadays/ these days + present simple

BODY (3 PARAGRAPHS)

List your causes + explanations/ examples ⮕ propose solutions ⮕ results of solutions

Paragraph 1:

- One of the main causes of the problem is that...

- By this I mean, ...

- For example, ...

- The solution is for the government to+ V // To tackle this problem, parents must...

- As a result, ...(a result of your solution to the problem)

Paragraph 2:

- Another cause is that...

- What I really mean by saying this is that...

- For instance, ...

- The way forward might be (for someone) to + V...

- Consequently, ...

Paragraph 3:

- A third cause of the problem is that...

- In other words, ...

- A good example would be that...

- Dealing with this issue involves + Object + V-ing…

- This would lead to ...

WAYS TO EXPRESS SOLUTIONS

- A solution is for the government to (+ bare inf.)

- To tackle this problem, people should (+ bare inf.)

- The way forward might be to (+ bare inf.)

- This problem could be addressed by (+ V-ing)

- Dealing with this issue involves (+ O + V-ing)

CONCLUSION

Summarize the causes of the problem & show your view about the topic + indicate who should solve the problem.

- All in all/ All things considered/ In conclusion/ To sum up,...

- ... it is clear that/ there is no doubt that (children's watching TV too much) is an increasingly worrying issue.

- In my opinion,/in my view, /As I see it,...

- ....the main responsibility for solving the problem lies with parents and governments

- Governments, parents, and schools all have a role to play in tackling the problem.

- Action must be taken urgently, otherwise, our societies will face even greater (health/education) problems in the future.

SOLUTION TO A PROBLEM STRUCTURE

INTRODUCTION

1.   Give Background

2.   Introduce the Issue

3.   Give a Negative Result

BODY PARAGRAPH #1 (2-3 reasons)

1.   Topic Sentence

2.   Reason

3.   Cause Expression

BODY PARAGRAPH #2

1.   Topic Sentence

2.   Solution

3.   Modal Verb

4.   Purpose

CONCLUSION

1.   Summarise Solutions

2.   Final Opinion

PROBLEM - SOLUTION SAMPLE ESSAY

TEMPLATE

INTRODUCTION:

+ Paraphrase the topic sentence of the task question

+ There are a number of reasons behind this point of view and several solutions should be proposed to .....

BODY

+ Body 1. Topic sentence 1: There are two primary reasons why ......

1. One reason is that ....

2. Another reason is that...

+ Body 2. Topic sentence 2: However, measures must be taken by governments and international bodies to......

1. Firstly,.. / The first solution would be ..../ One simple solution would be...

2. A second measure would be... / Furthermore,.../Also,...

CONCLUSION:

In conclusion, it is clear that there are various reasons for... (topic), and steps need to be taken to tackle this problem.

SAMPLE

Many people believe that international tourism is a bad thing for their country.

What are the reasons? Solutions to change negative attitudes.

<u>Model essay:</u>

It is widely argued that global tourism has a negative impact on destination resorts and countries. There are a number of reasons behind this point of view and several solutions should be proposed to change these oppositional attitudes.

There are two primary reasons why local residents often consider international tourism as a cause of serious problems in their countries. One reason is that it may have an adverse impact on traditional customs and indigenous practices because tourists may be insensitive towards the feelings of local residents. For example, some western tourists visiting developing Southeast Asian countries may be rowdy or wear unsuitable clothing, which might have an undesirable influence on the local young people who copy the immodest or provocative behaviour and fashions. Another reason is that tourists often pollute or litter beautiful spots and several famous beaches in Vietnam, such as Cua Lo and Sam Son, have been spoiled by this lack of respect for the local environment.

However, measures must be taken by governments and international bodies to change negative attitudes toward tourists. Firstly, the unquestionable economic benefits of international tourism for local economies ought to be more widely promoted through official media. International tourists spend money in shops and restaurants and create jobs in service industries and this aspect must be publicized. At the same time, tourist agencies should urge visitors to respect the local customs and culture of their hosts. Secondly, bodies such as the World Tourism Organization must enforce strict regulations on the tourism industry, ensuring that local operators are responsible for clearing litter and disposing of waste in ways that do not harm the environment, and issuing international Blue Flags to indicate clean beaches.

In conclusion, only by addressing the concerns of local people will negative attitudes to international tourism be changed.

IELTS EXAMINER COMMENTS

+ Task response:

Certainly, this essay meets most of the criteria for a very high band score. I would characterize your response as well-developed, with relevant, extended and supported ideas". Correctly, you did not try to discuss too many reasons for the problem [you focused on two important reasons in paragraph 2]. You will notice in my suggested version, that I have given more emphasis to examples, to avoid any danger of discussing the problems in a way that is too general. In paragraph 2, I found your example of the environmental problems of litter on some Vietnamese beaches really excellent to support your point. I would like to see another real-life "example" in paragraph 3.

+ Coherence and cohesion:

As always, you provided a well-organised essay. The logical paragraph structure is supported by precise topic sentences and clearly identified arguments. Sentences were well-linked.

+ Lexical resource:

There is some excellent vocabulary too: traditional customs and indigenous practices/heavily polluted due to littering/booming/hostile attitudes/fosters understanding and tolerance.....

+ Grammatical range and accuracy:

As with lexis, this area of your writing is strong. There is no problem with the range of grammar structures, which included a second conditional sentence, relative clauses and the consistently correct use of modal auxiliary verbs

USEFUL VOCABULARY

- **Widely argued:** widely refers to how many people have argued this same thing; if something has been widely argued, it means that lots of people have said the same thing about something; "it is widely argued that the key to success is to focus on specific goals and use your time wisely"

- **To have a negative impact on:** to have a negative effect on something; this means that it is not good for you; "procrastinating can have a negative impact on your level of productivity"; "spending all day on facebook can have a negative impact on your ability to finish your work"

- **Destination resorts:** a place where tourists like to visit on vacation; a destination is a place (like Hawaii) and a resort is a specific hotel or accommodation where people stay

- **Behind this point of view:** the reason for having this point of view; the underlying explanation for something; the reason why someone thinks the way they do; "behind this point of view is the understanding that success happens to those who are focused on the most important results"

- **Oppositional attitudes:** having an oppositional attitude means that you are against something, you don't support an idea, a policy or regulation; an attitude is how you think about something; "the democrats try hard to change the oppositional attitudes of the republicans towards Obamacare"

- **A cause of serious problems:** the reason why something terrible happens (the cause); serious (important, significant); problem (something bad); "smoking is known to be the cause of serious health problems"

- **To have an adverse impact on:** to have a negative/bad effect on something; "the war had an adverse impact on the environment, due to all the chemicals that were sprayed"

- **Indigenous practices:** indigenously refers to the people who are native to a local area; in the US. the indigenous people are the native Americans; practices are the traditions and customs of a culture; the things they do; "some modern people don't understand certain indigenous practices"

- **Insensitive:** not sensitive to somebody or something; it means that you don't notice what you are doing and the effect that it is having on a person or a place; "his father was insensitive to the fact that he was disappointed at not being able to travel with him to japan"

- **Rowdy:** noisy, loud, rough; "the boys were too rowdy last night and they got in trouble by the police"; "the athletes were so rowdy that the referees had to warn them several times"

- **Unsuitable clothing:** not suitable, inappropriate, not the correct or acceptable type of thing; "in the middle east, you will get in trouble if you wear unsuitable clothing, showing too much of your body"

- **To have an undesirable influence on:** to have an unwanted influence on somebody or something; to do something so that it influences someone in a way that is not wanted by somebody else; "the teachers were concerned that going to bars would have an undesirable influence on their students"

- **Provocative behaviour and fashions:** provocative means to cause annoyance, anger, or another strong reaction on purpose, like that is what you want to do with your behavior or clothing; provocative can also mean that it arouses sexual desire or interest; fashion refers to the clothing that you wear; "the young person was punished for her provocative behavior and fashions while attending school"

- **To be spoiled by:** to be ruined by; when something spoils something else, it means that it destroys it or makes it worse; "the lake was spoiled by the oil spill"

- **Lack of respect for:** to have no respect for someone or something; to not pay attention to agreed upon rules or customs; "young people these days have a lack of respect for the old ways"

- **Unquestionable:** without question; not able to be disputed or doubted; to describe when there is no question that something is a certain way; "knowing how to program computers is an unquestionable skill to have these days"

- **Widely promoted:** promoted in a big way; thoroughly or broadly; when you promote something widely you let a lot of people know about it; "the company widely promoted the release of the new Xbox"

- **To urge visitors to respect:** to advocate earnestly the doing, consideration, or approval of something; to press for; to try to get someone to do something; you urge someone to do or not do something; "they urged the visitors to respect the rules and not feed the animals"

- **To enforce strict regulations on:** to enforce means to make sure that people follow the laws or regulations by punishing them if they don't; strict means tough or tight; to enforce strict regulations on something means to make sure a punish people if they do something against the regulation; "the police had to enforce strict regulations on the people so that they would stop polluting the river"

- **Disposing of waste:** to get rid of the waste or garbage, usually by taking it to the dump or landfill; "the company was told that they were not disposing of waste properly, and they were fined $25,000"

- **Harm the environment:** to have a negative impact on the environment, like on the lakes, rivers, the air, etc; "everybody knows that chemicals from factories can harm the environment"; "if your company continues to harm the environment in this way, we will have to shut you down"

- **Addressing the concerns of local people**: to listen to what the people are concerned about and then do something about it; to address means to deal with or do something about something; a concern is a worry, something that you have negative thoughts about and you want something to change; locally refers to the people who live in the town or area; "the politicians said that they would start addressing the concerns of the local people related to the high levels of air pollution"

TASK 2 WRITING TYPE "2 PART QUESTION"

- Why is this the case? Is it a positive or negative development?

- What are the reasons? What are the effects on society and family?

STRUCTURE

• INTRODUCTION

+ Introduction topic (Paraphrase the question of the assignment)

Answering both questions given in the task   only giving out a general answer without giving details.

• BODY 1: Answer questions 1 in detail

• BODY 2: Answer questions 2 in detail

• CONCLUSION

Repeat the opinion given in the 2nd sentence of the Introduction part

2 PART QUESTION SAMPLE ESSAY

Nowadays, more and more people decide to have children later in their life.

What are the reasons?

What are the effects on society and family life?

Model essay:

In recent years, the decision of parents to start a family later in life has become an increasingly popular trend. There are a number of reasons for this trend, which is having a significant impact on both family life and on the community as a whole.

There are two important reasons why more people nowadays are deciding against having children when they are young. Firstly, rather than embarking on parenthood, many individuals consider that building their own successful careers is top-priority. If they had to split their time between working and bringing up their offspring when they were in the early stages of their careers, their performance at work and promotion prospects could be negatively affected. Secondly, delaying childbirth could give young people countless opportunities to enjoy their lives. For example, this choice may let young couples have a richer social life, pursue their interests and hobbies or even to travel the world.

However, this tendency could have negative consequences in terms of both family life and society. An important concern for a family is that raising children could be a huge challenge for older parents. Even though they might have a high socioeconomic status, as well as great experience and knowledge, it may not be easy for them to communicate with and relate to their children, due to the generation gap. Another negative factor is that getting pregnant after 35 years of age oftentimes carries more potential health risks. Specifically, this could increase the danger of having a miscarriage or stillbirth for older mothers, and babies might be at greater risk of having Down's syndrome. Consequently, this could negatively affect the quality of the future workforce.

In conclusion, there are a number of reasons why more and more people prefer giving birth later in life. As a result, there could be negative influences on individual families and the society at large.

IELTS EXAMINER COMMENTS

Task response:

This is an excellent essay with a lot of strong points. I have never seen this topic before. It is a very interesting one. In paragraph 2, you suggested two very relevant reasons for this trend. You explained both of them fully and you supported your second point with an example. In paragraph 3, you focused exclusively on negative impacts. You argued both points convincingly and at length, again giving real-life examples to support your ideas. My score for task response is 9 +

Coherence and cohesion:

The topic sentences were ideal. You identified your arguments perfectly in paragraph 2. In paragraph 3, you referred first to „the first impact'. I think that the identification of your second argument will be clearer if you write: „Another impact is....' This would be more effective than „Furthermore, ...'. As your sentences were also linked very smoothly, and for coherence/cohesion my score is 9 +

Lexical resource:

I think that one of the strong points is this essay is your awareness of words which combine together well („collocations'): to start a family, embarking on parenthood, embarking on parenthood, to split their time between...

Grammatical range and accuracy:

You use a range of structures both simple and complex. As with lexis, this area of your writing is strong.

USEFUL VOCABULARY

• **To start a family later in life:** to begin a family later rather than earlier; in the past couples used to start their families at younger ages, like 22, 23 or 24; nowadays they are having babies, which is how you start a family, in their late 20s or even 30s and 40s; "They decided to start a family later in life, preferring to work on their careers during their 20s and early 30s. They finally had their first baby when they were both 38 years old."

• **Increasingly popular trend:** increasingly means more and more so, as in something is happening more often, popular means that a lot of people are doing it; and a trend is something that a lot of people do at once, like a fad or a style; in this case it means that something is being done by more and more people at this time; "Taking a gap year before going to university is an increasingly popular trend among young people."

• **Having a significant impact on:** significant means to be important or notable; to have an impact on means to affect something in some way, either positively or negatively; "This heat is having a significant impact on our ability to work outside. It's just too hot! "

• **Community as a whole:** a community is a group of people, can refer to a small or large group of people, like a neighborhood, school or church community or as a large group of people, like a city, a culture, a nation of people; "The mayor wants to work with the community as a whole, rather than with just a few special interest groups here and there."

• **Deciding against:** to decide means to make a decision or a choice about something; against means to make a decision, not in favor of something; "They are deciding against going to Europe this summer. Instead, they are going to stay home and take summer school classes."

• **Embarking on parenthood:** to embark on something means to start something; in this case it means to become a parent; parenthood is what you call the role of being a parent; you are always a parent once you have children, but this refers to the time you spend raising them; childhood is they time period when you were a child; "They will be embarking on parenthood this summer, when their new baby is born."

•   **Top-priority:** top means the highest point and priority means something that you want to do more than other things, so top-priority means the thing you want to do the most, above everything else; "They think that making money is the top priority in their lives right now."

•   **To split their time between:** to split means to break into parts; in this case, it means to spend some of your time doing one thing and some of your time doing another thing, splitting your time into parts; "They split their time between New York and Los Angeles."

•   **Bringing up their offspring:** to bring up means to raise; this is what you do as a parent with your children; you educate them, nurture them, etc.; offspring refers to your children; "They are bringing up their offspring in a very strict household."

•   **Huge challenge:** huge means large or giant in this case; the challenge is very big; it's difficult or tough; "Raising children and working is a huge challenge that not everyone wants to undertake."

•   **High socioeconomic status:** your socioeconomic status refers to how much money you have and therefore your status or place in society; if it's high, it means you have a lot of money: "Even though they have a high socioeconomic status, they really aren't that smart."

•   **Generation gap:** the experience of not understanding your parents or grandparents and them not understanding you due to being raised during different time periods, in a different cultural setting; "They were able to bridge the generation gap by watching old and new movies together and discussing them."

•   **Negative factor:** negative meaning not good; factor is something that affects something else; a negative factor is something that you have to consider because it might not be good; "The one negative factor about this job is that I have to get up so early."

•   **Oftentimes carries more potential health risks:** oftentimes just means often or many times; to carry more potential risk means that it is possible to have health problems because of something; in this case, it is possible that a woman can suffer a health problem if she has a baby later in life, like after 35; "Undergoing certain procedures oftentimes carries more potential health risks than doing nothing."

- **Specifically:** used when you want to provide something specific, certain details about something or you want to say something very clearly; "She specifically said she did not want to work full time, just part time."

- **Having a miscarriage:** this is what happens when a woman does not carry the fetus to full term (a baby), it usually happens early on in the pregnancy; "She isn't worried about having a miscarriage."

- **Down's syndrome:** a genetic chromosome 21 disorder causing developmental and intellectual delays; "Even though their child has Down's syndrome, they are so happy to be parents and they love her very much."

- **Consequently:** used to say something that happens because of something else; something is a consequence or result of something else; "She didn't study for her test; consequently, she failed."

- **Future workforce:** refers to the fact that young people will be workers in the future; "The future workforce will face new challenges never experienced before."

- **Negative influences on individual families:** negative meaning bad; influences meaning effects; on individual families refers to each nuclear family - a couple and their children, rather than families in general; "Based on the research, the negative influences on individual families could be lessened with more support from the government."

- **The society at large:** people in general; the community as a whole; "Violating human rights doesn't just affect individuals, it affects the society at large

2 PART QUESTION SAMPLE 2

Many museums and historical sites are mainly visited by tourists but not local people.

Why is this the case and what can be done to attract more local people to visit these places?

Model essay:

It is true that tourists from many parts of the world pay more visits to museums and historical places than local inhabitants. There are many reasons for this, but this situation should be addressed by attracting locals in some practical ways.

There are two main reasons why museums and historical sites are preferred more by tourists than by local residents. One reason is that museums are too familiar to the locals. If museums do not change anything, there will be nothing new for the locals to discover. Like eating the same dish every single day, they feel bored with visiting the same places. Furthermore, entrance tickets at some historical sites are expensive for the local inhabitants to afford. For example, in Dien Bien, a province in northwestern Vietnam, it is rather hard for the residents to make ends meet, let alone to spend money on visiting some famous historical attractions there.

The government should take some measures/steps to tackle this issue effectively. Firstly, museums ought to be invested in more by the authorities to refresh the exhibits. The fresher the exhibitions are, the more local residents will be interested in them. Secondly, historical relics need to be free for all the local people. Without worrying about additional expenditures, residents will pay more to visit historical sites in order to broaden their knowledge about their hometowns.

In conclusion, there are some known reasons for this trend. However, something should be done by the authorities to attract more visitors from the local areas

(252 words)

IELTS EXAMINER COMMENTS

We could consider it a '2-question essay' or a 'problem-solution essay'. In practical terms, it makes no difference. You did the correct thing - you used one paragraph to answer each question.

You put forward two clear and strong reasons why more locals do not visit museums and historical sites. You explained both of these and used a great example [Dien Bien]. In paragraph 3, you suggested solutions for both of these problems in turn. I cannot think of any better or clearer arguments than those which you used. This was the other part of your essay. The techniques that you used showed that you had planned and organised your answer carefully.

Again, there is nothing that I would change: the paragraph structure [as we have already noted] is logical and the topic sentences indicate perfectly the main idea in each paragraph. Your arguments are signposted clearly for the examiner: you used ***One reason/Furthermore*** in paragraph 2 and ***Firstly/Secondly*** in paragraph 3.

As you developed your explanations, the sentences linked perfectly with each other, using varied sentence structures and natural, fluent language.

USEFUL VOCABULARY

- **Pay more visits:** to pay a visit just means to go to some place, to make a visit, to visit

  Example: they have been paying more visits to museums ever since they decided to learn more about art.

- **Historical places:** places that have historical value due to some important events in the past

  Example: on their trip to Cambodia, they visited a variety of historical places, including Angkor wat.

- **Local inhabitants:** the people who live in the town

  Example: the local inhabitants do not enjoy having so many tourists in their town.

- **Practical ways:** a way of doing something that has practice value, that is rational or logical

  Example: the book I read talked about many practical ways to lose weight. I am going to try some of them.

- **Rather hard:** quite difficult, used express that something is indeed hard example: I find it rather hard to study more than four hours per day.

- **Make ends meet:** to make enough money to pay all the bill

  Example: he has been having a hard time making ends meet over the last few months.

- **Take some measures/steps:** to do something to address an issue, like to create a rule, a law or a regulation

  Example: the government needs to take some measures to reduce air pollution in the city.

- **Refresh the exhibits:** bring in new works of art or other to show to the public

  Example: the museum curator likes to refresh the exhibits every two months.

- **Additional expenditures:** expenses that are in addition to other basic expenses

  Example: the additional expenditures will total $10,000 by the end of the project.

- **Broaden their knowledge about:** to learn more about something

  Example: the students will broaden their knowledge about other cultures by traveling to other countries.

- **Known reasons:** reasons that people already know about, that they are familiar with

  Example: there are many known reasons for the lack of interest in electoral politics, like the fact that only rich people can run for president.

- **Attract more visitors:** to get more people to come to visit

  Example: one of the goals of the museum this year is to attract more visitors from neighboring towns and villages.

OUTLINE FOR OPINION ESSAY
(AGREE/DISAGREE)

INTRODUCTION

Clearly state your agreement/ disagreement & rewrite the original question in your own words

Concerning the issue of (topic)/ it is believed that (topic question)/ As far as I am concerned/ Personally,...

- *I am in favor of/ completely agree with* the statement for several reasons which will be given out in this essay.

- *I do partially/ totally disagree with* the statement for several reasons which will be given out in this essay.

BODY (3 PARAGRAPHS)

List your arguments + explanation/ examples.

Paragraph 1:

First of all, it can be said with certainty that... *(your argument).* The key explanation is possibly *because ... For example,...*

To begin with, there are obviously a number of motives *surrounding* this idea ... *(your argument).* By this I mean, ... *For example,*

Paragraph 2:

Secondly, a special consideration is that... *(your argument).* The main basis is probably because ... *For instance,*

In addition to this, a subsequent could be because ... *For instance,*

Paragraph 3:

Last but not least, ... *(your argument).* This is because . . . . *A good example would be that...*

Counterargument + Refutation

- Those who *disagree*, on the other hand, point out that there are a couple of shortcomings ...Those who *object to* this opinion may claim that... *(+ contrasting viewpoint)*

- Those who *support/favor* the proposal of.... may argue that... *(+ contrasting viewpoint)*

- *Opponents of the ideas say that...Others may argue that...Other are of the opinion that...Other people put forward the view that...*

HOWEVER,...

- I am unconvinced that... /I don't believe that... *(your argument + reasons)*

- It is hard to accept that...There is little evidence to support the ... that...It is unjustifiable to say that...The problem with this argument is that... *(your argument + reasons).*

- Perhaps this is true, but it cannot be denied that... *(your argument + reasons)*

Ex: *Other people put forward the view that* playing online games can enhance children's creativity *because they think that* in order to win the game, the children have to come up with the best strategies or tactics, which is good for their brain developments. *However, perhaps this is true, but it cannot be denied that* they are more likely to get addicted to these games than focusing on their study and homework. Consequently, they would get bad marks or fail their examinations.

Pattern 1	Pattern 2	Pattern 3
• Thesis statement	• Thesis statement	• Thesis statement
• PRO idea 1	• CON(s) + Refutation(s)	• CON idea 1 — Refutation
• PRO idea 2		
• CON(s) + Refutation(s)	• PRO idea 1	• CON idea 2 — Refutation
	• PRO idea 2	
• Conclusion	• Conclusion	• CON idea 3 — Refutation

		• Conclusion

CONCLUSION

Briefly summarize your arguments & re-emphasize your opinion

- *All things considered,* there is no absolute answer to the question of...

- *Taking everything into consideration,* it is unlikely that ..../it is possible that.

- *In conclusion, ...//To sum up, ... I think/ believe/ I am of the opinion that...*
  because of.....

OPINION STRUCTURE

INTRODUCTION

1. Give Background

2. Introduce the Issue

3. Give a Negative Result

BODY PARAGRAPH #1

1. Topic Sentence

2. An Example

3. A Result/ Purpose

BODY PARAGRAPH #2

1. Topic Sentence

2. An Example

3. A Result/ Purpose

BODY PARAGRAPH #3

1. Topic Sentence

2. An Example

3. A Result/ Purpose

CONCLUSION

1. Summarise Main Points From Paragraph 2&3

2. Final Opinion

DISCUSS + OPINION

- Discuss both views and give your opinion

- Do the advantages outweigh the disadvantages?

- Discuss the advantages and disadvantages and give your opinion

What is the difference between "balanced opinion" and "discuss both views and give your opinion" ???

- Balanced opinion: both views are YOUR views → you shouldn't talk about "some people" or "other people"

- Discuss both views and give your opinion: you can talk about "some people's/other people's" views

TEMPLATE

INTRODUCTION:

Paraphrase the topic sentence of the task question

+ While there are benefits to ….., I would argue that

BODY 1: On the one hand…

BODY 2: On the other hand, I believe that ...

CONCLUSION:

In conclusion, it seems to me that...

SAMPLE ESSAY

Some people think that it is best to live in a horizontal city while others think of a vertical city. Discuss both views and give your opinion.

Model essay:

Some people believe that living in a horizontal city is the best, while the opponents of this idea prefer to settle in a vertical city. While there are benefits to residents who dwell in a city which consists of low-rise construction, I would argue that cities with skyscrapers and high-rise buildings offer more advantages.

On the one hand, it is beneficial for residents to live in a horizontal city based on a few financial and security reasons. Firstly, people have to pay less for building services. If residents settle in a private house, they may save a great deal of money since they will not have to pay for building services. Secondly, living lower to the ground is safer for inhabitants when emergencies occur. For example, if a fire starts in the home, they can quickly escape from the dangerous areas because the building is not too high off the ground and it will not take much time to leave.

On the other hand, it seems to me that living in a vertical city is the best choice. A city with skyscrapers will have more space for public usage because there will be less land used for residential areas due to the amount of people who can live in high buildings. As a result, the government would be able to use this land to build hospitals, schools or places for entertainment. Furthermore, it is much more convenient for residents to live in an apartment in a tall building which offers a wide range of goods and services, thanks to shopping malls and service centers on lower floors.

In conclusion, while living in a horizontal city does have some benefits, it seems to me that the advantages of life in a city with skyscrapers makes living in a vertical city the better choice

(300 words)

IELTS EXAMINER COMMENTS

+ Task response:

This was an interesting task question. To be honest, I have not seen this topic before. You answered the question fully. I cannot improve on the technique which you used. You stated your position clearly in the introduction and consistently throughout the essay. The beginning of paragraph 3 and your conclusion were the ideal places to re-state your opinion. All the points which you mentioned were relevant and fully developed and I have to give a score of 8.5 for this section.

+ Coherence and cohesion:

Your paragraph structure was, as I have already mentioned, clear and logical.I then looked at your topic sentences. These indicated expertly the central idea in each paragraph. I, therefore, scored 9

+ Lexical resource:

The language meets the criteria (natural and appropriate) . The essay contained some good topic vocabulary: low-rise construction/skyscrapers and high-rise buildings/building services/thanks to shopping malls and service chains on lower floors.

+ Grammatical range and accuracy:

You certainly used a good range of grammar, including adverb clauses, relative clauses, conditional forms, comparatives and other useful constructions. So, this section again achieves a maximum score.

USEFUL VOCABULARY

- **Opponents of this idea:** opponents are people who disagree with an idea; they are against an idea, a policy or a rule; they don't support it; they want something else to happen' "the opponents of this idea believe that it won't be good for the public"

- **To settle in:** to decide to live in a specific place; to decide to move to an area and stay there; "they have decided to settle in new york"

- **Based on:** to be the reason for something; "their decision was based on years of experience"

- **Financial and security reasons:** financial refers to money issues, like paying fees; security refers to safety, like being safe in your own home in terms of crime or emergencies

- **Private house:** private describes the fact that you own the house, and therefore you make all decisions about it and pay for repairs and maintenance yourself, versus paying apartment or condo fees

- **Lower to the ground:** to be close to the ground, which makes it easy to get out in case you need to leave the house quickly due to an emergency

- **Dangerous areas:** an area that is not very safe, that is not secure, for various reasons

- **To take much time to:** this phrase talks about how long something takes to do; it will or will not take much time to do something

- **Best choice:** the thing that you should choose to do because it is the best option

- **To have more space for public usage:** to have more land available for building public buildings, like government offices or parks, etc.

- **Due to:** the reason for something; "due to the overwhelmingly positive responses, the company decided to release another version of the iPhone"

- **Much more convenient for:** used to describe when something is much easier for somebody to do compared to something else; "it's much more convenient for them to come to my house first and then go with us to the restaurant"

- **Thanks to something or somebody:** used to express the idea that something is good because of something specific; "thanks to my dad's help, we were able to purchase a new home"; "they were able to finish the project on time, thanks to the assistance they received from their boss"; "she got an A on her paper, thanks to the feedback she got from her tutor"

- **The better choice:** used when you are comparing things, there may be several good choices, but one is clearly the better choice, better than all the others; can be used interchangeably with the best choice

VOCABULARY FOR ACADEMIC IELTS WRITING TASK 2

VOCABULARY FOR THE OPINION PART

- In my opinion......

- I think.....

- I strongly agree with the idea that.......

- My opinion is that.....

- I strongly disagree with the given topic....

- In my view.....

- Apparently.....

- I believe.....

- From my point of view.....

- Personally speaking.....

- To my way of thinking.....

- It seems to me that.....

- To me.....

- I feel that.....

- It appears that.....

- I suppose.....

VOCABULARY TO SHOW COMPARISON

- Likewise.....

- In the same way.....

- Similarly.....

- Similar to.....

- Like the previous point.....

- At the same time.....

- Also.....

- Just as.....

VOCABULARY TO SHOW CONTRAST

- On the other hand.....

- However.....

- On the contrary.....

- But.....

- Oppositely.....

- Nevertheless.....

- Alternatively.....

- While.....

- On the other hand.....

- Whilst.....

- Unlike.....

- Even though.....

- In contrast to this.....

- Alternatively.....

- Then again.....

VOCABULARY TO SHOW AN EXAMPLE

- As an example.....

- For example.....

- For instance.....

- To show an example.....

- Like.....

- Namely.....

- Such as.....

- As.....

- Particularly.....

- In particular.....

- As an evidence.....

- To illustrate.....

VOCABULARY TO SHOW CONSEQUENCE, EFFECTS OR RESULT

- As a result.....

- As an effect.....

- Consequently.....

- So.....

- Thus.....

- Therefore.....

- Hence.....

- The reason why.....

- For this reason.....

- Thereby.....

- Eventually.....

VOCABULARY TO SUM UP

- In short.....

- To sum up.....

- In a word.....

- That is to say.....

- To put it simply.....

VOCABULARY TO MAKE A POINT STRONG

- Thought.....

- Although.....

- Nevertheless.....

- Nonetheless.....

- Yet.....

- Still.....

- Must.....

- Even if.....

- After all.....

- Thus.....

- Therefore.....

OTHER TRANSITIONAL WORDS / CONNECTIVE WORDS

- Then.....

- Otherwise.....

- Else.....

- As soon as.....

- Besides.....

- As much as.....

VOCABULARY FOR THE CONCLUSION PART

- In conclusion.....

- To conclude.....

- In summary.....

- On the whole.....

- To sum up.....

- To conclude with.....

- To summarize.....

- All in all,

- In short.....

- Overall.....

VOCABULARY FOR GENERALISING A STATEMENT

- Generally.....

- In general.....

- Generally speaking.....

- All in all.....

- Overall.....

- As a rule.....

- On the whole....

- All things considered.....

VOCABULARY FOR EXPRESSING CONDITION

- Provided that.....

- Providing that.....

- If.....

- Unless.....

- For this reason.....

- Because of that.....

- In case.....

- So that.....

VOCABULARY FOR EXPRESSING AGREEMENT

- I completely agree that.....

- I strongly agree.....

- I quite agree that.....

- I agree with the opinion that.....

- I totally agree with the given idea that.....

- I could not agree more.....

- I am quite inclined to the opinion that.....

- I concur with the group who believe that.....

- I accept the fact that.....

- I accept that.....

- I am in agreement.....

- I approve the idea.....

- I consent that.....

VOCABULARY FOR EXPRESSING DISAGREEMENT

- I strongly disagree.....

- I disagree with the opinion that....

- I completely disagree with.....

- I disagree with the statement.....

- I totally disagree with the given idea that.....

- I disagree with the group of people.....

- I quite oppose the opinion that.....

- I totally do not accept the fact that.....

- I disapprove that.....

- My own opinion contradicts.....

- However, my opinion is different.....

VOCABULARY FOR EXPRESSING PARTIAL AGREEMENT

- I agree to the given statement to some extent…..

- To some extent…..

- Up to a point I agree…..

- In a way…..

- More or less…..

VOCABULARY FOR EXPRESSING CERTAINTY

- Definitely…..

- Certainly…..

- Of course…..

- No doubt…..

- Without any doubt…..

- Doubtlessly…..

- Undoubtedly…..

VOCABULARY FOR ADDING FURTHER INFORMATION

- Furthermore…..

- In addition…..

- Moreover…..

- And…..

- Similarly…..

- As well as…..

- Also…..

- Besides…..

- What's more…..

- Likewise…..

VOCABULARY FOR PRESENTING TIME OR SEQUENCE

- First/ Firstly…..

- Second/ Secondly…..

- Third/ Thirdly…..

- Final/ Finally……

- Last/ Lastly…..

- At the same time…..

- Then…..

- Meanwhile…..

- As soon as…..

- Since…..

- After this / that…..

- After…..

- Before…..

- While…..

- During…..

- Simultaneously…..

- When…..

- Following this…..

USEFUL WORDS TO SHOW RELATIONS:

Across, across from, where, in which, to which, from which, under, over , inside, on top of, along, through, as far as, northern, southern, eastern, western, to the left/ on the left hand side, to the right/ on the right hand side, to the south, in back, behind the, in front, in front of the ..., in the middle, adjacent, mid point halfway, interior, diagonal, edge limit, parallel, parallel to, perpendicular to, opposite, overlapping, exterior, intersection, rectangle, square, circle, vertical, horizontal.

USEFUL WORDS FOR CLASSIFICATION:

Aspect, attributes, bases, basic kinds of, categories, characteristics, classes, classifications, classify, contradictory, contrasting, dissimilar, distinguishable, divide, divided into, factors, falls into, fundamental, important, insignificant, kinds of, main kinds of, methods, minor, mutually exclusive, opposing, opposite, origins, parts, primary, secondary, qualities, significant, similar, sources, types of, unimportant.

USEFUL WORDS FOR DEFINITION:

Aspect, Category, characteristics, clarify, class, condition, define, definition, explain, explanation, form, in other words, kind, method, paraphrase, type

THE WORLD FAMOUS LIST OF THE MOST COMMON WRITING MISTAKES MADE BY STUDENTS IN THE IELTS EXAM

1. Do **not** use (...) (etc) when writing a list. Instead, lists of examples should follow the pattern; (A and B)... (A, B, and C),.. (A,B,C, and D). For example: phones, radios, televisions, and other forms of technology.

2. Do **not** ask the reader any **questions** in your essays. For example; "How do you think we can solve the problem of over-crowding in cities?"

3. Do **not** use **exclamation points** in your essays. For example; "In my opinion, it's the best solution to over-crowding in cities!!"

4. Phrases like **"more and more"**, **"bigger and bigger"** are too informal. Instead use structures such as **"much more"**, **"a great deal larger"**. Also, **"big"** is too informal for reports and essays. Use **"large"** **"sizeable"** **"significant"**.

5. Do not begin sentences with **"And"**, **"But"**, **"Or"**. Instead use linking phrases such as **"In addition"**, **"However"**, **"Since"**, **"As a result"**.

6. The first sentence of each body paragraph should be a topic sentence, it should define the content of the paragraph in general terms.

7. **"Most/almost"**: **"Most"** is art adjective (usually) which means the greatest quantity, amount, measure, degree or number of something. It is followed by a noun, prepositional phrase or adjective;. "Most people", the most popular" "Most of his time".

8. **"Almost"** is an adverb which means very nearly, all but, slightly short of, not quite, Examples: "We're almost home.", "almost finished", "almost every house", "almost never" "almost all of the students".

9. Manage your time well. **Task 1= 20 minutes. Task 2=40 minutes.** A poorly written essay for report will receive a higher band score than an incomplete one. **Task 1 = 150 words, Task 2 = 250 words.** Make sure you write the minimum number of words.

10. Subject-verb agreement: He, she, it....plays, does, receives, negotiates, etc. This is a rule you learned in elementary grammar. You cannot still be making this mistake on the IELTS test. If you make this mistake in your essay, you can forget about getting a good band score.

11. Use the correct verb tense. This is another elementary mistake that will keep you from getting a good band score Pay attention to every verb you write and consider what tense you should be using. In addition, memorize past forms of irregular verbs.

12. Articles **(a, an, the, no article):** The last of the three biggest elementary mistakes. Review the rules about articles and apply them to every noun you write.

13. Singular/Plural, Countable/Uncountable: When speaking in general about something, use the plural form. For example: "**People** use **computers** in their **offices** every day."

14. In essays, **no personal opinions** in the body paragraphs, only in the introduction (for thesis-led) or conclusion. Use **impersonal opinions** in the body paragraphs.

15. Write your essays from a **global perspective**, because the questions are asked from a global perspective. Try to avoid relating the essay question only to Vietnam. It should be about the world in general.

16. Use linking words and transition phrases at the beginning of all body paragraphs, most sentences in the body, and the conclusion. For example; Firstly, On the other hand, In summary.

17. No contractions; for example: "shouldn't" = should not

18. Keep pronouns out of the essay body paragraphs. Words such as, you, we, I, should be omitted or written as people, students, society.,.

19. Active tense can be changed to passive tense to omit the pronoun..

20. **Effect** is a noun. **Affect** is a verb.

21. In the introduction, do not tell us what you're going to do. For example: "In this essay I will compare…" This essay will show both the positive and negative benefits…" Instead write a concise thesis statement.

22. Avoid using **absolutes** such as; all, every, none, only, always, never, completely, totally…

23. Don't use the word "thing", Name the object or action you're writing about.

CONCLUSION

Thank you again for downloading this book on *"Shortcut To Ielts Writing: The Ultimate Guide To Immediately Increase Your Ielts Writing Scores"* and reading all the way to the end. I'm extremely grateful.

If you know of anyone else who may benefit from the informative tips presented in this book, please help me inform them of this book. I would greatly appreciate it.

Finally, if you enjoyed this book and feel that it has added value to your life in any way, please take a couple of minutes to share your thoughts and post a REVIEW on Amazon. Your feedback will help me to continue to write the kind of Kindle books that helps you get results. Furthermore, if you write a simple REVIEW with positive words for this book on Amazon, you can help hundreds or perhaps thousands of other readers who may want to enhance their life have a chance getting what they need. Like you, they worked hard for every penny they spend on books. With the information and recommendation you provide, they would be more likely to take action right away. We really look forward to reading your review.

Thanks again for your support and good luck!

If you enjoy my book, please write a POSITIVE REVIEW on amazon.

-- Johnny Chuong –

CHECK OUT OTHER BOOKS

Go here to check out other related books that might interest you:

English Collocations In Use: Master 500+ Collocations Explained In 10 Minutes A Day

http://www.amazon.com/dp/B01JHUNYZQ

Productivity Secrets For Students: The Ultimate Guide To Improve Your Mental Concentration, Kill Procrastination, Boost Memory And Maximize Productivity In Study

http://www.amazon.com/dp/B01JS52UT6

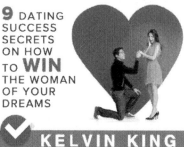

http://www.amazon.com/dp/B01IOHIPNY

http://www.amazon.com/dp/B01IO1615Y

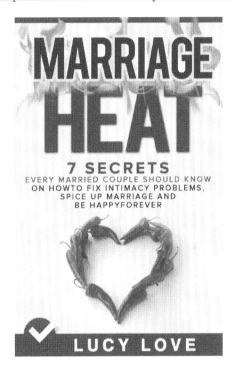

http://www.amazon.com/dp/B01ITSW8YU

http://www.amazon.com/dp/B01HS5E3V6

http://www.amazon.com/dp/B01J7G5IVS

Printed in Great Britain
by Amazon